KU-216-082

Mama Tina

By the same author
Bridge Across My Sorrows (with Robert Coram)

Mama Tina

The Inspiring Sequel to
Bridge Across My Sorrows

CHRISTINA NOBLE

with
Gretta Curran Browne

JOHN MURRAY

© Christina Noble 1998

First published in 1998
by John Murray (Publishers) Ltd,
50 Albemarle Street, London W1X 4BD

The moral right of the author has been asserted

All rights reserved. No part of this publication may be reproduced in any
material form (including photocopying or storing it in any medium by
electronic means and whether or not transiently or incidentally to some other
use of this publication) without the written permission of the copyright
owner, except in accordance with the provisions of the Copyright, Designs and
Patents Act 1988 or under the terms of a licence issued by the Copyright
Licensing Agency, 90 Tottenham Court Road, London W1P 9HE.
Applications for the copyright owner's written permission to reproduce any
part of this publication should be addressed to the publisher.

A catalogue record for this book is available from the British Library

ISBN 0 7195 5638 4

Typeset in Bembo by Servis Filmsetting Ltd, Manchester

Printed and bound in Australia by
Griffin Press Pty Ltd, Netley, South Australia

To my Mammy. You left us the greatest gift of all, love.

*To the children of the world. Without you
we wouldn't have a world.*

To my children, and my cherub grandson, Thomas.

To my son, Thomas, never forgotten.

*To Michael and Shirley Hunt, truly great friends
who were instrumental in putting my home, life and
family back together again.*

*To Wendy Evans, for her total dedication to
the children of Mongolia.*

*To Hazel Wood. We shared so much and
the memory will live on.*

CONTENTS

ILLUSTRATIONS

The author and publishers would like to thank Lucy Forward for giving her permission to reproduce Plate 10, and Richard Shears for permission to use his photographs.

ACKNOWLEDGEMENTS

So MANY PEOPLE and organizations from across the world have supported the Christina Noble Children's Foundation in so many different ways that if I were to thank you all individually it would be a book in itself. I thank you here from the depths of my soul. Because of you thousands of children are now able to live as children, enjoying a real childhood and a sense of hope for the future. I want especially to thank all the people who have sent me gifts and beautiful letters. I wish I could have replied to each of you, but I have been working non-stop. Without your support and care neither I nor the Foundation could carry on.

A few people I must single out. Our International Chairman Peter Williams has been a supporter and friend since his years as British Ambassador to Vietnam. Thanks also to Carol Wolfson, her husband Michael Garvey, and to Ernst & Young, who have done so much to help the Foundation.

To Henrietta Schaffer and Peter Spiers of the Schumacher Foundation I owe a huge debt of gratitude for their continued moral and financial support. I don't know what I'd do without them. Thanks also to Unesco for its interest in the Foundation, and especially to Dieter Barestricher.

To His Excellency Brendan Lyons, Ireland's Ambassador to Malaysia, I send special thanks for all his understanding and help. Special thanks also to all the staff of the British Consulate in Vietnam for their help and understanding, and to Lord Wise of King's Lynn for his support.

The Foundation has so many helpers worldwide that it is impossible to name them all, though every single one of them is important. Special thanks go to Dr Sandra Short and all the team who never stop working for the Foundation in Australia, and to Vivian Easton – thanks, Vivian, for being a pal. Special thanks to Lindsay Farr and Geoff and Ute Glenn for really caring for me and for your selfless love for the children.

I send a huge thank-you to the people of Ireland for their warmth and generosity, and especially to Ronnie Delaney, Barbara Donnelly, Oona Linnehan, Marjorie McHenry, Isabel Ryan, Lorraine Sweeney and Una Henry – also to all the very special volunteers who helped me during my tour across Ireland. And special thanks to Paddy and Maura McKillen for giving us an office in Dublin and for their constant support for the young students.

Thanks also to Vets with a Mission and to all the other wonderful people in America who have given us their support; to Kati Somers and Pats Cornelius in Belgium; to Asa Ekroth in Switzerland; and to Raymond Laas, President of CNA in France.

For accommodating the Foundation in London I am indebted to Hardy Oil and Managing Director John Walmsley. Especial thanks to Graham Hearne OBE, Chairman of Enterprise Oil, and Director of Corporate Affairs Ray Dafter. Many thanks to Emma Jellicoe and Christine Dafter for their hard work in the London office; also to Katie Cardona, and to Justin Coldwell, Laura Lindsay and David Pirkis of the London

Board, and to Joe Woolf and Ray – I know I must have driven you mad at times, Joe, but thanks for listening.

To Wendy Evans in Mongolia a special thank-you – you've been a tower of strength to the children, Wendy, and we're all going to miss you.

My thanks also to Tim Bond, who has been an enormous support and has helped me in so many ways.

My thanks go also to His Excellency Huynh Ngoc An, Vietnamese Ambassador in London, and in Vietnam to Mr Nghiem Xuan Tue, Minister Mrs Nguyen Thi Hang and Ms Thien Huong at the Ministry of Labour, Invalids and Social Affairs, and to all the staff at the Christina Noble Children's Foundation in Ho Chi Minh City for their hard work, under-standing and support.

To all my family – my brothers and sisters, Andy, Michael, Kathy, Sean and Philomena, my children, Helenita, Androula and Nicolas, and their partners, Craig, Michael and Sara – I give my love. What you mean to me goes too deep for words.

To Caroline Knox, my editor and friend, who has never once lost patience during our work together, a special thank-you for your tolerance and your belief in me.

To Gretta Curran Browne for helping me write the book and bringing it forward.

And finally to Hazel Wood – I don't know how to thank you, Hazel, for your help with the book. What you did was fantastic.

*Some of the children's names have been changed
to protect their identities.*

Prologue

W HEN I'M ON one of the fund-raising tours which are now a big part of my life, someone in the well-dressed audience will occasionally ask me about my philosophy. What is our approach at the Foundation? I try to answer, but often the two worlds I'm moving between – people who have nothing and people who have everything – seem so far apart that it's hard for me to explain one to the other. Perhaps the best way I can do so is by telling you the story of a little Vietnamese boy called Phuc. When I feel a gentle breeze on my face it always makes me think of him.

My work with the poorest of the poor takes me into some of the worst areas of Saigon, or Ho Chi Minh City as it is now officially called. It was in one of these that I first came across Phuc and his family, down by the railway tracks in Nhieu Loc, the city's canal district, a place more squalid than any shanty town, where people live in constructions like cages, one on top of the other.

In the midst of this congestion I noticed something that looked like a small coal-box – just a few boards of broken wood nailed together. I might have mistaken it for just that had it not been for a piece of old curtain hanging over the entrance. As soon as I saw that, I knew there was a woman inside.

I pulled back the curtain, peering into the blackness, and I was hit by the foul stench of human flesh. A family of five were hunched inside: a father and mother, two little girls and a young boy of about ten. The box was no more than four feet square, smaller than many Western toilets. So small, in fact, that there was no room to lie down – the family had to sleep sitting up against the walls.

My eyes went to the boy because, unlike the others, he was not sitting but lying on his back, motionless, with his matchstick legs drawn up towards his chest. A closer look told me he had cerebral palsy.

I was appalled by what I saw. Even the streets and alleys would have been a much healthier place to live. Tears sprang to my eyes and I wanted to be sick, but I knew I mustn't: it would only add to the humiliation these people were already feeling. So I swallowed hard and fought back my emotions.

I was with my Vietnamese colleague Helen Thuong. 'Helen,' I said, 'please ask the father if I can speak with him.'

The father came outside. He was about thirty-five, very neglected-looking and thin. The mother and children looked neglected and worn down too, but the father looked worse. Instinctively I knew that if there was any food to share, he was the type of man who would let his wife and children have most of it. I was struck by the pain in his eyes and the lack of hope in his voice when he spoke to me – his low self-esteem.

My first reaction was to do something immediately, to take them out of this hovel, this box, but I knew it was impossible. 'Could you come to the Children's Centre at 38 Tu Xuong

Street in District 3?' I asked him through Helen. 'I think we might be able to help you.'

He looked somewhat taken aback, but with great dignity he nodded and said 'Yes'.

I asked him if I could see the whole family. Very politely they came outside. The two little girls, ragged but beautiful, stood looking at me, mystified by this yellow-haired stranger who was talking to their father. The father carried the little boy out, and I was immediately struck by the tender way he lifted and held him. I could see that he often did this by the way the boy's arms automatically went round his father's shoulders. The little boy's name was Phuc, we were told.

Then I saw the back of Phuc's head. It was not rounded, as it should have been, but almost flat. Phuc had spent all his short life lying on the ground. His body was twisted from head to foot and as frail as a five-year-old's.

Phuc's parents came to my office that afternoon. 'Please sit down,' I said. I could feel their embarrassment, and I understood it only too well. The Vietnamese are a gentle people, but they are very proud, and this family were obviously the victims of circumstance. I explained to them that I too had been very poor when I was a child. I too had lived in terrible conditions with my own brothers and sisters.

'Please don't be embarrassed,' I said, 'just tell me, how can I help you? What do you need most?' I felt almost silly asking. I could see that this family needed everything.

The father said quietly, 'I need a job.'

'What kind of job? What can you do?'

'If I had a Honda-om,' he said, 'I could be a Honda-om driver,' but he shrugged as he answered, as if it was an impossible idea. He didn't even have food, never mind his own taxi.

'Okay,' I said, 'let's talk tomorrow. Could you and your

family be at my office by half past ten? I'll send the Foundation van to pick you up, if that's all right with you.'

'Yes, yes,' he said, without any hesitation this time.

Next morning, at 8.30 a.m. prompt, we had a meeting of the Foundation staff. The group included Mr Hai, our accountant; Luong, our book-keeper; our three Vietnamese social workers; and Miss Anh, the sponsorship co-ordinator. Also present were Lucia Ennis, the assistant manager; Christine Byrne, the volunteer co-ordinator; my daughter Helen; Dr Hanh; and Helen Thuong, our Vice-Director.

Helen Thuong chaired the meeting since she had already met the family and could explain the situation to the staff in Vietnamese. Then we started the brainstorming.

Mr Nam, the senior social worker, was the first to speak. 'Before we do anything we must check out their story, Mama Tina, to make sure it's true. How do we know they don't have a house they rent out while they're living in that box, or something else like that?' Nam knows his job, and takes it very seriously. I always find him very reassuring. As an orphan and a former street child he has the same eagle-eye and experience as myself. He also has a great soul and a good brain.

'I know what you're saying, Nam,' I said, 'but believe me, these people are genuine.'

'The father says he wants a job,' said another of the social workers, Ngoc, 'but it seem he has no qualification. I think the idea of a Honda-om is a good one. Now we have many motor cars and trucks in Ho Chi Minh City and the traffic so very bad, I see many foreigner taxi on the back of Honda.'

Everyone nodded in agreement.

Luong, our book-keeper, spoke up. 'Yes, Mama Tina, I think this is a good idea, because now not many cyclos can go into the city like before, not since Government change the law. It is true, many people now use Honda-om for taxi.'

'I think we all agree', said Helen, 'that a Honda-om is the best way to start helping this family. If we buy one quickly, the father can start work straight away.'

At this point I called for Quoc, our minibus driver, to join the meeting. He came in and sat down.

'Quoc,' I said, 'they've all agreed that Phuc's father needs a Honda-om. Do you think it's a good idea?'

Quoc answered with his dolphin-like smile, 'I think very good, Mama.'

'Now, Quoc,' I said, 'I'm going to ask you to go out and find one, secondhand and in good condition. Maximum price eight hundred dollars. But I'll be expecting you to bargain hard and do a deal.'

'Oh, no problem, Mama, no problem,' Quoc assured me. 'I know where I can find.'

The rest of us continued to discuss the family's situation. We all agreed that housing was a priority, and that for the sake of their health we had to act fast. There was no way any decent person could leave them living in those conditions. But could we *afford* to rent them a big room, putting down at least one year's rent in advance?

I looked across at Mr Hai, our accountant, a man always in control, never fazed. 'Well, Ma'am,' said Mr Hai, 'you always say to us, if we don't have it, we must find it. And I say to you, Ma'am, we can do. Yes, we can afford.'

'I love you, Mr Hai,' I said, 'you always make me feel good.' Everyone smiled as I planted an affectionate kiss on Mr Hai's cheek while he blushingly protested, 'Oh Ma'am, you always do like that.'

'That's because I love you,' I said. 'And because you always give me good answers.'

At half past ten little Phuc and his family arrived. Again, I couldn't keep my eyes off the father as he carried Phuc in. He was so loving and tender. Helen and Dr Hanh and I told the parents about our meeting and asked them what they thought. It was difficult for them to take in what we were saying.

'We would like to arrange for Phuc to go to our Physiotherapy Unit in Phuan Nuang District for an assessment,' I said. 'If he goes, Dr Loc there will take good care of him.' In Vietnam there is neither the knowledge nor the equipment to care for children with cerebral palsy, but I was hoping that Dr Loc might be able to suggest some kind of long-term rehabilitation programme for Phuc.

The father and mother agreed, surprised and obviously delighted that finally something might be done for Phuc. They also agreed that they and the little girls would have a medical check-up at our health clinic. But when I offered to look after Phuc full-time at the clinic until I could find them a room, they both shook their heads. It would be for only a matter of weeks, I explained, until we could find them other accommodation, and in the meantime we could give Phuc proper nourishing food. I understood when their answer was still 'No'. Phuc was their son and they wanted to take care of him themselves.

It was coming up to lunchtime now. There were a lot of other children to see and two emergency situations to deal with. The humid tropical heat was intensifying, so I asked Nam to take the family to lunch. I didn't manage any myself because Quoc was back with a long list of bikes and prices.

'Mama, Mama, I see Vespa, three hundred dollar.'

'Three hundred dollars? How old is it?'

'Is very nice, Mama, but I not sure if it last long. It twenty years old.'

'Did you see any others?'

'I see many, Mama, one very nice Honda, no same like father Honda dream, but good Honda, maybe ten years old.'

'How much?'

'Five hundred dollar.'

'Five hundred! Are you joking?'

'Yes, Mama, I think bike very good. But I see better one for seven hundred dollar, only seven years old.'

After a lot of humming and hahing I said, 'Okay, let's go for that one.'

'Yes, Mama, I think same.'

He was off like Flash Gordon and returned in no time with a blue bike. It looked very decent and Quoc had been assured that the engine was good. If it was, I felt it was seven hundred dollars well spent.

I made a quick cup of tea, had a cigarette and put my swollen feet up for five minutes. I sat thinking, as I so often do, 'If only I could win the Lotto! There are so many children out there like Phuc . . .'

Nam arrived back with the family. I could see all the Vietnamese staff looking at us, just as excited as I was. They're such a great crowd the staff, so concerned and always happy when we can give someone a new chance.

We went downstairs to where Helen Thuong and a beaming Quoc were waiting with the Honda. When we gave it to Phuc's father he just stared at it. At first he was amazed but then he looked suspicious. I gave him the papers and suddenly his face broke into a huge smile.

'I hope it will earn money for you,' I said. 'Give you some independence.'

Down in the courtyard we said goodbye. The whole family crammed themselves on to the Honda, with Phuc strapped to his father's back, and they rode off, with the two little girls waving and giggling. The staff and I just stood smiling at one another. There was no need to say anything.

In bed that night I thought and thought about the family. Next morning our Vietnamese Assistant Manager, Dan, did a lot of checking out of land and prices. Then I made a phone-call to a man who had just sent us a large donation. He insists on remaining anonymous, but I don't know how the Foundation would survive without him, he is so generous.

I told him about Phuc and his family and asked if we could use some of the money to buy land and materials so the family could build their own home. 'That money is to help the children however you think best,' he said immediately.

On Tuesday I saw Phuc's darling little face again when he came back to the office with his Mom and Dad and his two sisters. I gave him a kiss, and he put his hands around my face and hung on to the hair over my ears. He was smiling, *really* smiling. I looked at Phuc's mother and our eyes met – she was beaming, I was beaming.

I told Phuc's parents that we had found a piece of land just outside the city. It was cheap, about $2,000, with a little green field around it. We invited them all to come out in the van with us to see it and give us their opinion. It was their choice. Then we all piled into the van for the half-hour drive. There was a tremendous sense of excitement. I was holding Phuc in my arms and telling him and the two little girls where we were going. The children couldn't understand what I was saying but they knew from the way I was saying it that it was something good.

'Quoc, put a bit of music on,' I called over to Quoc in the driving seat.

The first tape Quoc put on was an Irish song, 'The Fields of Athenry'. It's a song I always call 'Michael', because it reminds me of my eldest brother. Quoc's a very sensitive young man and he knows it's my favourite song, though I can hardly bear the line that goes: 'Michael, they are taking you away . . .'. It has too many memories for me.

The van left the city behind and we turned off the main road into a country lane. We stopped and parked. The children pressed their faces against the window, staring out. I wondered what they were thinking. I handed Phuc to his father, and the little girls and I held hands and skipped through the grass to the little plot of land. Their parents followed with Phuc, and while they were talking to Helen, I took him in my arms again. He was moving his head from side to side, squinting up at the vast blue sky, gazing up at the great arc of blue, utterly transfixed. He had never seen such space or light before.

I laid him gently down and guided his hands over the grass while his little sisters stood staring at him, obviously amazed. Phuc was pulling at the grass, feeling it, holding it, his fingers exploring with incredible intensity. There was a gentle wind blowing and he seemed to be bathing in it, almost as if he could see it and touch it. His head, his eyes and his whole face were moving. It was as if, after ten years of lying in the dark like a corpse, Phuc had come to life.

I left the family and walked away across the fields. At moments like this I thank God for the dream that guided me to Vietnam. I feel that I'm the one who has been given the greatest gift.

The family liked the plot. With help from volunteers they built their home within a month and moved into it. Phuc's mother takes great pride in the little business she now runs, selling her home-grown flowers from a roadside stall. His father goes into the city each morning to work with his blue Honda-om, and when he has some spare time he helps us at the Foundation.

Physiotherapy and a good diet have done a lot to ease Phuc's condition. Last time I saw him at the Foundation he was in his snazzy new wheelchair and he was wearing a baseball cap just like any other cheeky ten-year-old. He and his sisters have the chance to be children now.

So I'd say my philosophy isn't just about mending bodies. It's about restoring people's independence, giving them a life, not just an existence. It's about respect and love and dignity. Those are the things we owe our children. Children are the ones who need them most of all.

Out of the Shadows

ONE

T HE FIERCE MORNING sun is scorching my head and arms as I ride my new blue Chinese bicycle through the Saigon streets. My pedalling becomes slower and more laborious. What I desperately need is a lovely long, ice-cold drink to cool my burning forehead and ease my parched throat. It's 1989 and I've been in Vietnam only a few months.

I park my bicycle outside a café, lock it and hurry inside. It's not a café I've ever been in before and as soon as I see the shelves behind the bar I wish I'd found it earlier. They're stacked with row upon row of rare Coca Cola cans. Oh God, what surprise and joy! I've always loved Coke and I drank gallons of it when I was in England. As I stand waiting to be served I can already feel the sweet, metallic taste on my dry tongue.

The Vietnamese man behind the counter is dressed like a hotel manager – white shirt and black bow tie. He gives me a beautiful smile.

'Sweetheart, will you give us one of those cans of Coke,' I say, 'before I faint from this heat?'

He goes on smiling at me, but at the same time he shrugs. 'Seventy-five,' he says with a sigh. 'Seventy-five . . .'

I'm mystified. It doesn't sound like the price of a Coke. 'Seventy-five dong?' I ask him.

Still smiling, he lifts down two of the red Coca Cola cans and shows me their pierced lids. Then, with infinite sadness, he turns them upside down and shakes them. Not a drop. All the cans are empty.

I'm not just disappointed, I'm annoyed. '*Empty!* So why do you have them up there on the shelf?' I demand.

'Americans, seventy-five,' he sighs. 'Americans go, Coca Cola go. Long time, long time . . . No Americans, no Coca Cola . . .'

Suddenly I realize what he's talking about – *nineteen* seventy-five – the year the last Americans left Vietnam. For him, these shelves of empty Coca Cola cans hold his memories of a Saigon that is past. Memories that linger on to this day. But it isn't only memories the Americans left behind.

It's 1998. Once again it's been a scorcher of a day, with the temperature well up into the nineties. But now the cool of the evening has arrived, and I'm out pedalling my old blue Chinese bicycle through the streets. I stop at Café 19, a busy, popular place, just off the famous Dong Khoi Street right in the centre of Ho Chi Minh City, which is what we should now remember to call Saigon.

Inside the hubbub of Café 19 a waiter recognizes me. 'Mama Tina! Hello-lo'! he yells, and instantly brings me a Coke. Since the trade embargo was lifted in 1994 it's no longer a rare commodity.

Occasionally I bring some of our Sunshine children to this café for a Coke – each delicious glass filled to the brim with ice. When the children ask for a second glass I shake my head, pretending to be angry. 'Do you think I'm a millionaire?' I say.

'I've spent so *much* today. Next time I'll only be able to afford half a bottle each.' The children giggle, they're used to me saying that. But sometimes funds are so low that a 'bottle between two' really *is* all I can afford. It's a tiny treat, but to children with so little, it means so much.

This evening, however, I'm alone. I finish my drink and chat for a minute or two to the waiter in my limited Vietnamese, which is Saigonese overlaid with a strong Dublin accent. The waiter has never come across half the invented Vietnamese words I use, yet he understands me completely. At the door of the café we say goodbye and I mount my bike and cycle off towards Pham Ngu Lao.

Pham Ngu Lao is a favourite haunt for street children selling flowers, postcards, stamps, chewing-gum, shoe-shines – beautiful children in faded shorts and T-shirts with skinny brown arms and legs. They're great little sales people who think it's *real* smart to bargain with you for an extra cent, and if they get that extra cent, the triumphant smile they give you is irresistible.

Yet, above all the enterprising gaiety and good food and bright lights a dark shadow falls – there's more to bargain for in Pham Ngu Lao than flowers and postcards.

I cycle on, half-listening to the rock music blaring out from somebody's speaker. Then I see them as I turn the corner – two adorable little girls, street children with pretty dirt-streaked faces. Instantly I'm alert: a Western man and a Vietnamese cyclo-driver are bending down talking to the children. I'm certain I know why. I quickly get off my bike and pretend to be checking the wheel-chain, covertly watching, waiting to see what's going to happen.

The Western man climbs into the bucket seat of the cyclo and the driver lifts the two little girls and places them on his lap. Like a bolt of lightning I throw down my bike and run forward, glaring at the Westerner. 'Who are you and where are you taking these children?' I demand.

He looks astonished, then frightened. He's breaking the law and he knows it. 'You needn't tell me where,' I say, 'because you're not taking these children *anywhere*.' I bend down and lift the little girls from the cyclo but the driver pushes me away. Furious, I push him back and try again to lift the children out, but the driver lunges and blocks me.

I turn to the Westerner. 'If you want to know who I am,' I say, 'I work for the children of Vietnam, and if you take these children away I'll report you to the police. You too!' I warn the cyclo-driver. 'I'll report you too, you bastard!'

By now a crowd has gathered. The driver suddenly jumps on his bike and the cyclo starts moving with his customer and the children on board. I pull him off and another pimp on a Honda starts threatening me. I yell back, screaming my threats so that everyone in the crowd will know what these men are up to. In the midst of all the shouting the Westerner suddenly throws the children to the ground, jumps off the bike and runs into the crowd. Within seconds he's disappeared.

The cyclo-driver is obviously livid. He grips the two little girls' shoulders tightly. I try to reason with him, but he's not having any of it, and of course I know why – the children are part of his business.

The second dealer is back now with a young Vietnamese man and woman squeezed on to the pillion of his bike. He claims they're the children's parents. A feeling of hopelessness engulfs me. Years of experience have taught me all the tricks of this game. As surely as I know my own name I know that these two little girls are being sold into prostitution, but there is nothing I can do but hand them over to the two people who claim to be their parents.

I fumble in my pocket for my card with the address and telephone number of the Foundation. I ask the 'parents' if they'll consider coming to my office there to discuss how we might help them and the children. Yes, they'll come they say. Maybe tomorrow, maybe the next day.

I stand and watch them all walk away. As they go one little girl turns her dirt-streaked face and smiles back at me, her small hand waving in farewell. She's only about five, and clearly she's bemused by all this adult attention. I wave and smile and blow her a kiss, but inside my heart is breaking. I know she has no idea of the horror she has just escaped – a horror that may still be waiting for her.

The cyclo-driver is glaring at me – if looks could kill I'd be dead, but I'm too upset and furious to care. I get on my bike and cycle off down the long, garishly lit street wondering if I'll ever see those two little girls again. Hoping against hope.

Yes, the Americans left Vietnam in 1975, but it's true to say that the memory of them is still everywhere. Even today you have only to walk down Dong Khoi Street and you'll see traders and street children selling souvenirs which they claim are relics the Americans left behind. The most common are square metal zip lighters with sentimental inscriptions engraved on the case:

No journey is too far for me to come back and find you.

Saigon you stole my heart.

The deepest ocean in the world is shallow compared to the depths of my love for you.

Many of them have a date scratched on the case, like this one, dated January 1975 – the year the last of the Americans left:

19

Wait for me under this light by the Majestic Hotel at 8 every morning and one day we will find each other again . . .

Did she wait for him by the Majestic Hotel, I wonder. And did he ever come back – even years later perhaps, as a tourist? How poignant these memories are. But nothing in the American legacy is more poignant than those victims of their country's destruction – the children.

When I arrived in Vietnam in 1989 I found a country forgotten by the rest of the world. After reunification with the North, thousands of people from the cities in the South were encouraged to give up their homes and move into the countryside to become self-sufficient as farmers. But the land was too poor, too devastated by chemicals, and the experiment failed. Many died of malnutrition and those who were left flooded back to Saigon – a tide of the dispossessed, living hand-to-mouth in the streets and alleys. I had never seen poverty or homelessness on such a scale.

Now the trade embargo which the Americans imposed after the war is lifted, and in 1997 the US Secretary of State, Madeleine Albright, came to Vietnam to lay the foundation stone of a new American Embassy, a move that was greatly welcomed. She also announced that America is to fund research into the effects of Agent Orange, that deadly defoliant used in the Vietnam War, which devastated the countryside and produced terrible deformities in generations of Vietnam's children.

Now, in 1998, Saigon is a fast, modern city with a whole new skyline. Bicycles, pyjamas and slippers have been replaced by Honda motor-cycles, Western-style designer T-shirts and jeans, business suits, mobile phones and fashionable leather shoes. The once dark nights now glow with the lights from discothèques, big international hotels, expensive restaurants and designer shops.

The change is incredible. But there is still another, darker side to Saigon, a nightmare place of starvation and squalor and broken families. Abandoned children live, and frequently die, alone on the streets, and there is now a growing market for young children as prostitutes. As countries like Thailand crack down, the demand from these hideous sex-tourists becomes more intense. They are cunning, manipulative, and experts at winning children's trust, despite the government's very real attempts to stamp out this terrible trade.

For some time the government's response to the street children was to round them up and remove them to detention centres outside the city. That has gradually changed, but now, with tourism booming, these children are at the mercy of something far worse.

So in this new Vietnam, as in the rest of the world, it is those with the least power, the children, who suffer. To most Vietnamese these children are known as the *bui doi* – the 'dust of life' – and they are trampled like dust by an adult world that's only out for its own profit. It is to these brave children that I have dedicated my life and it is for them, and for all the other uncared-for children of the world, that I am telling my story.

TWO

A LITTLE NAKED girl was running towards me. She looked imploringly at me as the bombs exploded around her on the cracked dirt road, and held out her hands to me. Shining in brilliant white letters above her was one word. *VIETNAM.*

Every time the dream that had haunted me swam to the surface of my memory I felt fear. I carried it around with me as I walked the streets during those first two weeks after my arrival in Saigon. What was I doing here, I kept asking myself. Who was I? What was I? No background, no real education, no knowledge, standing in a country I knew nothing about – not the language, not the culture – nothing but a dream.

So much had happened in the years since I had first had that dream. When I dreamt it, one night in 1971, my life was simply a struggle for survival, and it truly was a question of life or death. At that time I was married to a man who abused me as I'd been abused all my life. In the course of my childhood I'd been orphaned, abandoned, raped, and imprisoned in institutions. In the years of our marriage Mario took away any shred of self-respect I had left. But he gave me the greatest possible gift, my three wonderful children. For that I will always be grateful to him.

Escape from a violent marriage wasn't easy then. There were no local refuges for battered wives in the early 1970s, and although I had tried to leave with the children many times, there was nowhere I could go. Mario was very cunning with money, he was very threatening and he had very threatening friends. He beat me with anything that came to hand when he was in a rage, he broke my nose, and my blood frequently spattered the walls. By 1976 I felt sure that one day he would go too far and kill me.

He terrified the children but he never hit them. Helen, my eldest daughter, kept begging me to leave. She was ten, Androula was eight and Nicolas was six. A little ten-year-old begging her mother to go away: I felt my heart was breaking, but I knew I had to go. I also knew that I would never, never abandon my children.

That terrible decision, once made, was the start of my own healing. It had been a long and painful process, and it wasn't over yet. Sometimes I felt it was only just beginning. That period of my life took me through the valley of the shadow, through breakdown and depression, through mental hospitals and therapists' rooms, and through courts where I fought to regain my children. But during those years I never forgot my dream.

In 1989, when I had reached calmer waters, I received a letter from a friend who knew of my interest in Vietnam. 'The streets are overrun with destitute children. They need help,' he wrote to me from Saigon. It was a kind of confirmation of what I believed my dream had been telling me. I had been a street child myself. I had known the life that these children were living. My dream was calling me to help them, and now, at long last, I was ready.

But now I was in Saigon I wasn't so sure, and my confidence began to ebb. In 1989 there was a sense of dereliction everywhere. Homeless people sheltered in neglected empty buildings. Paint was peeling and the pavements were crumbling.

I felt desolate as I walked the streets. People would often look at me strangely, a blonde Westerner, wandering alone through parts of the city where foreigners were rarely seen. It wasn't homesickness. I had so much homesickness as a child that I've never allowed myself to feel it again. I've never allowed myself to get attached. But I missed my children in England and I kept thinking about them. Sparkling fair-haired Helen, a musician and like me in so many ways. Lovely, dignified Androula, with her dark eyes and beautiful dark hair. Nicolas, my handsome son, who was always so kind and thoughtful. They were young adults now, I kept thinking. They had come through a lot and they were well able to manage without me. But like any mother I worried about them and held them in my heart. I'd already been through the anguish of leaving them once. And now to leave them again for the sake of a dream . . .

Perhaps the dream was silly, I told myself. What could I do here? The very air of Saigon then was permeated with suffering and loss. I felt as if I'd gone back in time to my childhood in Ireland, to the poverty and hopelessness I remembered in the Liberties. These were the people I'd grown up with, the dispossessed of the world. Everywhere I went I saw people with missing limbs, hopping, one-legged without a shoe, or holding out their one arm to me, trying to sell me something. There were people with no arms, people with no legs dragging themselves along, people whose bodies looked like one huge burn. I felt as if I was in hell.

I saw such despair on the faces of the mothers carrying tiny babies at their breasts, with young children pulling at their arms. Their eyes were hollow and the skin on their cheek-bones and round their eyes was pulled and drawn. The babies looked to me like little chicks without nests, their mouths wide open, crying for food, and yet there was no food, nothing in the breasts that hung like empty sacks, and no place for nesting. The mothers' faces told me that for them this was the end of the road. I kept feeling their anxiety, imagining what it must be like to be a mother with a newborn and nothing to give. I wanted to fix things for them now, I didn't want them to suffer any more.

One woman I recall particularly, standing on the corner of one of the main streets, Dong Khoi. She was haggard and wasted, her hair was tangled, and she had a baby on her shoulder and two small children clutching at her legs. Yet there was a dignity about this woman. I sensed that she came from an educated background, probably one of those families that had moved out into the government's new 'economic zones' in the countryside and then been forced back into Saigon, only to find themselves in oblivion, a family that had lost everything in the war. She looked as if she was in a fog, as if she had nowhere to turn. Yet I could feel that she didn't want to beg.

I saw the same dignity in many of the Vietnamese faces around me. Though they were in a hopeless situation, somehow these were not hopeless people. They had survived a war which was the greatest manmade ecological disaster the world has ever known. I felt humbled by their courage, and angry, very angry, at the terrible injustice of it all.

Whatever my doubts I knew I just had to find a way to do something. If I went back now to my normal life this vision of hell would haunt me, and I knew I'd never be able to live with myself. I knew what suffering was. I was inside these people and they were inside me.

But I felt frustrated. I just couldn't see what to do next. I didn't know anyone. I didn't belong to anyone. I didn't even have my darling dog Ty for company. In the mornings I walked the hot streets with their strange, pungent smells, or sat in small cafés, trying to accustom my ear to the unfamiliar sounds of the language. In the long afternoons I went back to my room at the old French colonial Rex Hotel in Nguyen Que Street and lay on my bed, my hands under my head, staring at the ceiling across which the odd, well-nourished cockroach lazily wove its way.

At night my sleep was troubled. It was as if all this pain was causing an eruption of my own past life, bringing the pain of my own childhood to the surface. In the early mornings I woke exhausted, drained, as if I had been crying for days. One night I dreamt that I was in a strange country. I was in a great space and people were sitting on seats all around me. They were kindly people, and I was moving, running, singing, yodelling, my voice making a strange liquid sound in my throat – 'aaaaah, aaaaah'. As I woke I realized it was the sound of my own screaming. Tears were pouring from me like a waterfall. I was mourning the losses and griefs of my past as I had never been able to mourn them before.

One torpid afternoon I'd fallen asleep on my bed at the Rex and when I looked at my watch again it was nearly half past four. I got off the bed and went down to the hotel restaurant for a cup of tea. The big room was empty at that time of the afternoon, apart from me and two young Vietnamese musicians sitting on the opposite side, a girl with a cello and a young man with a violin.

They were playing Strauss's *Blue Danube*, over and over, over and over, and as I sipped my tea the music went round and round in my head and I was back in Marrowbone Lane in the Liberties in Dublin, a scrawny street child singing with the other kids a horrible little rhyme we put to the tune of *The*

Blue Danube: 'It's all on my leg, gick, gick, la, la. It's two inches thick, gick, gick, la, la . . .' So long ago now, and yet as clear as if it were today.

For the first time I took in the full opulence of the restaurant, the faded magnificence of its decor. A huge cane blind covered the large window overlooking the street and on it was printed, incongruously, a crude reproduction of the Mona Lisa. Her gaze seemed fixed on me and I closed one eye and stared back at her and thought, 'What the hell are you doing here, Mona Lisa? You don't belong here, and neither do I.'

I left the restaurant and walked down to the ground floor of the hotel, which at that time was in an area of run-down, dilapidated buildings. As I stood on the steps of the hotel, I glanced instinctively across the road. Over the past few days I had become aware of two little girls, crouched on the other side of the road, digging in the dirt between the cracks in the concrete.

Both the girls had a typically Vietnamese beauty – jet black hair, enormous eyes – but their hair was dull and matted and their delicate skin was sallow from malnutrition and neglect. The smaller one had an endearing, gap-toothed smile. Every day, as I'd approached the hotel's main entrance and looked across at them, they'd also looked at me, holding out their hands to me, their eyes seeing only a foreign lady with yellow hair who could afford to stay at the Rex Hotel. An American, I expect they thought. Every day I had wanted to go over to them and take their outstretched hands in my own, but some fear had held me back.

They were there now, crouched in the dust. It was then that I realized they were not just playing there. They were digging up ants and putting them in their mouths. They were *eating* them. They both lifted their heads and gazed at me. I couldn't hold back any longer. I went over to them. I stood a few feet away from them as I spoke. I was still afraid.

'What are your names?' I managed to ask. Huong and Hang, they told me. Then Huong reached out a small grubby hand towards me. She held up both arms, as if asking for a cuddle. Our eyes met. I stretched my hand towards hers and our fingers touched. In that first touch I knew that my fate was sealed. I put my arms around her. There was no going back now. My dream of working for the poor children of Vietnam had become a reality.

THREE

My MEETING WITH Huong and Hang was a turning-point. Through them I met the street children. I'd hear reedy little voices calling 'Mama 'tina! Mama 'tina!' as I came out of the Rex Hotel. 'Christina' was too much of a mouthful, so that was what I'd become. I began to feel like the Pied Piper as the two little girls and their friends waited for me and went with me on my walks.

Most of the children spoke a little English, and gradually I began to get to know more about them and their lives. Some of them survived alone on the street, some lived on the streets with their families, and some of them had some sort of home to go to at night. Most of them sold chewing-gum, sweets or shoe-shines till the early hours around the clubs and hotels. Some of them stole to survive. There was a constant fear of the government vans.

These little people were children but they had no child-hood. Many of them, even the tiniest, were the breadwinners of the family because their parents weren't able to work. They were the mothers and fathers of their mothers and fathers. Truc, who was seven, spent his time like a little donkey, pulling

29

his crippled father through the streets on a board. Thai, who was eight and lived in a shack by the river, was the family breadwinner because his father was blind and his mother was too ill to work.

Another little boy, Giu, had come into Ho Chi Minh City from his starving province lying on the roof of a train. He lived on the benches near the Floating Hotel with his friend Luong, and the two of them looked out for one another. Sometimes I'd see them washing themselves in the pool near the Tran Hung Dao statue, rubbing away at the grime that was ingrained on their skinny bodies. They always gave me a cheeky grin, and for a minute you could imagine they were like any other ten-year-olds, until you saw that Luong had an ugly scarred stump for an arm.

I came to recognize the children who were living unprotected on the streets at night by the scabby infected mosquito bites on their arms and legs. One child I have never forgotten, though I saw her only once before the street crowd swallowed her up. She was trying to beg, and she was carrying her little brother slumped over her back. The child on her back was so painfully thin that you could see the bones in his skull, and his stick arms were hanging limply down on either side of his sister's shoulders. From the drugged look of him he had been given something to stop him crying. His eyes and lips were a mass of weeping scabs and sores, and there were bald patches of ringworm on his head. From time to time the little girl would push her small hip out and hoist the child up higher to give herself a break. I kept thinking: 'She must be so tired. My God, my God, what can I do? How can children be living like this?'

The sight of all these children was breaking my heart. Looking into their faces I saw myself, dirty, hungry, back in Marrowbone Lane in the Dublin Liberties all those years ago.

A gutter in Vietnam's no different from a gutter in Dublin, I thought. I remembered how I'd longed for treats, chocolates that the other children brought to school, and sometimes I'd take some of the street kids for an ice-cream with the little money I still had. On occasion I even smuggled them into the hotel, but before long the management was getting complaints from some of the well-heeled Russians who were staying there.

By this time what I was seeing was making me angry. Not just angry but furious. When the manager came to me with these people's complaints I looked straight at him and said, 'These are Vietnamese children. Are you going to throw them out and let the Russians stay?' The manager's attitude to me changed after that. But what was I doing? It seemed like putting plasters on gaping wounds.

Then I had another encounter that was to change my life. I've always believed that God was guiding me the day I first came across the centre for malnourished orphans, and met its director, Madame Nguyen Thi Man. I can't say I'm religious in the conventional sense. I never could be after all the cruelty I've seen the Catholic Church inflict on children in God's name. But I do a good bit of talking to the Man Upstairs.

I'd been walking and walking through the streets. It was almost as if I was looking for something, and eventually I found myself a little way from the city centre, in District 3. I remember my first sight of the sign that said Tu Xuong Street. It was quite a long street, with a few small cafés down at one end, and a high wall running down one side with big government buildings and some crumbling old colonial façades behind. There was a big green gate with peeling paint in the wall and I could hear the sound of children crying beyond it.

I approached the surly security guard. Then the small, erect figure of Madame Man appeared. She looked sternly at this strange Westerner who was asking to come inside, but she allowed me in. I shall never forget the sight of the bleak wards we walked through, full of tragic little bodies, and Madame Man's quiet answer to my horrified question. This was what war and famine had done to the children of Vietnam.

The place, I discovered, was government-run, and its official title was the Centre for the Rehabilitation of Malnourished Orphans. But there was little money then in that sad, devastated country to do anything much but give the children a roof. I remember standing in the dingy entrance, rooted by the horror of what I had just seen. It was then that I spotted the derelict building in the compound yard, and for the first time since I'd come to Saigon I knew what I had to do. As I looked at the place where the derelict building stood I had a vision of building a children's centre, a place where the forgotten children of Vietnam could get help for their damaged bodies, where they and their families would be accepted and treated with love. It seemed impossible, but I knew that I passionately wanted to do it.

Madame Man looked at me with her dark eyes as we discussed the derelict building and my idea. I could see she was sizing me up. 'You are very rich woman from the West?' she asked. 'I'm not a rich woman', I said. 'All I've got is a few hundred dollars and you can have that. What I want to do is help the children.' We walked around the compound together, looking up at the big, dark buildings on either side, talking and talking. 'I believe you will do it,' she said after a while. From that moment Madame Man gave me her support. There were only two problems. I had no money and, as she pointed out, I didn't have the government's permission either.

By this time I was existing on the few dollars I'd got left and I was living in a damp, cockroach-infested room in Le Loi Street. Madame Man kindly moved me into a small room in the compound at 38 Tu Xuong Street. It wasn't the Ritz by any means and the roof above my head leaked when it rained, but it was heaven compared to my slit-trench in Le Loi where at night, to get inside, I had to do a very sophisticated dance routine over the sleeping bodies of homeless people in the hallway.

In Le Loi Street I was often greeted by rats when I arrived. They were so bloody cheeky and self-assured, they didn't even lift an ear or flick a tail when they saw me coming. The rats were the best nourished occupants of that building. In fact they were so plump I thought they must all be pregnant.

Safe now in Tu Xuong Street, with pen and paper in hand, I sat on an old wooden bench in my room and set about trying to put down my reasons for wanting to build a medical centre for the sick and abandoned children of Vietnam, and why I thought this was necessary.

But before I could do anything I had to get the government's permission to work with children, and Vietnamese law required that I work with a government-approved partner. As I soon discovered, you cannot do anything without the government's permission in Vietnam. Tiny Madame Man had fought with the Vietcong and had influence in government circles. She insisted I go to Hanoi and explain myself. I must show the authorities that I wasn't just a rich Westerner with a bad conscience.

I was worried about spending money on a ticket to Hanoi. It was going to cost about $180, and I had to go on finding the money to live, so every cent mattered. But now the doubt about what I should do had gone. I wasn't going to let anything stand in my way, so I decided to take Madame Man's advice. Within a week I was boarding a plane to Hanoi. So much seemed to hang on this interview, and I felt apprehensive about meeting the grey-faced men at the ministry. As we boarded the ancient Russian plane I noticed its tyres had no tread left. Then I wasn't just anxious, I was scared stiff.

Safely landed, however, I stood before Mr Tue and his colleagues at MOLISA, the Ministry of Labour, Invalids and Social Affairs. It was a highly polished sort of office and behind Mr Tue's head was a beautiful glass-fronted cabinet of a dark reddish brown that I thought must be rosewood. In it was displayed a magnificent gold-fluted porcelain tea-set painted with exquisite flowers. I couldn't keep my eyes off that tea-set, it was the tea-set of my dreams. At home in Dublin we used to drink our tea out of condensed milk cans with the labels soaked off, but what I'd always longed for was a lovely little light china cup. As I stood before Mr Tue, that tea-set seemed to me to sum up the two extremes in the world.

My heart was beating furiously. Mr Tue and his colleagues smiled at me and shook my hand very warmly and invited me to sit down at the long table. The Vietnamese never show obvious suspicion, it would be too impolite, but I could sense that they were curious. They were trying to work out who this strange woman was who had just walked in like this on her own.

I half sat down and launched in straight away. 'Look,' I said, 'I want to work with the children. I know you don't know me. I know I'm supposed to have a lot of papers to show you, but I don't. I've only got a great love and understanding for the poor because my own life was very poor. I don't expect you to believe me. I don't expect you to trust me. I don't have anything to negotiate with but my heart. I'm putting that on the table. Can we negotiate with that?'

At first it seemed they hadn't heard me, or that they weren't sure if they'd heard correctly.

'Your heart?' said Mr Tue. 'Negotiate with your heart?'

'Yes,' I said.

Mr Tue and his colleagues spoke to one another in Vietnamese. From time to time they smiled at me and there seemed to be a softer look on their faces.

Mr Tue inclined his head. 'What is it that you want to do?'

At least they weren't telling this madwoman to get out. I was grateful to them for that, and it's something I've never forgotten. So I told them a little about myself, about my mother's death and my childhood in Dublin.

'There's something inside me that tells me I've got to help the children,' I said. 'It's not something I can explain to you, but I know I can do it. I just need you to let me. Even if you don't trust me, give me the benefit of the doubt, and if I break your trust you can do whatever you have to do.'

If I didn't get this permission I wouldn't even be able to begin. But how could I find the right words? What if these bureaucrats said no? I could feel the tears welling up inside me and I started crying. 'Please let me do this,' I said. 'I can't explain it to you. I just have to do it.'

'How would you do it?' asked Mr Tue.

'I'd build a kind of centre to help the sick children,' I said, 'the ones whose mothers haven't any milk for them. We could give them food and we could treat their illnesses. We could help them to get a life together with their mothers.'

My vision of the centre began to make me feel more confident. 'I'd like a place where kids could play in the day and maybe go home in the evening,' I said. 'Forgive me if I can't explain all this to you in a way you're used to hearing. I don't have an education but I do have a lot of courage and determination and I don't give up easily.'

'What would you call this centre?' asked Mr Tue.

'A Medical Centre,' I replied.

Mr Tue and his colleagues were obviously interested, but there seemed to be a difficulty here. 'We are the Ministry of

Labour, Invalids and Social Affairs,' said one of them. 'We are not Medical.'

'You could call it "Medical and Social Centre",' suggested Mr Tue unexpectedly.

'Brilliant,' I said. 'We could get around it that way.'

'You have money to do this?' Mr Tue asked.

'No,' I said. 'I've only got my heart, like I told you. Could I just take it one step at a time and see what happens?'

There was a lot more talking in Vietnamese. Then Mr Tue turned to me again.

'We think, Miss Noble, yes, you can try to do this. It is okay for you to do this, working with Madame Man.'

I almost leant across the table and hugged him. Instead I said 'God bless you', though later it came to me that, being a communist, Mr Tue wouldn't believe in God.

So that same day I was handed a red-sealed document giving me official permission from the Vietnamese government to work, not only with the children of Ho Chi Minh City, but with all the children of Vietnam. Madame Man was to be my government-approved partner.

As I flew back from Hanoi I couldn't quite believe it. Fancy letting me in there at all, I thought. These high government officials had put their trust in someone who in Ireland had been seen as the scum of the earth. I felt there really must have been divine intervention.

FOUR

I HAD NEVER raised funds, and quite frankly, I didn't have a clue where to begin. There were only a few expatriates in Ho Chi Minh City at that time, and as far as I could see they lived a sheltered life in the better-off parts of the city. People who knew about my friendships with the street children probably saw me as a complete oddball and I expect some of them thought I was mad.

However, I set about writing letters to foreign businesses on a battered old typewriter, and before long I had my answers. Every single company said no. It was obvious they saw the street children as a lost cause – and not one they wanted to be associated with either. There was just one exception. A man called Les Blair of Enterprise Oil invited me to come and discuss my project.

We met in the roof bar at the Rex Hotel, and as soon as I saw Les Blair I knew he was a man with a soul. He was big and gentle with a soft Glaswegian accent and lively brown eyes. I sensed that he had a lot of clout at Enterprise, but I was immediately struck by the courteous, respectful way he spoke to the waiter as he ordered our drinks. Les was not one of

37

those expats who saw himself as superior to the Vietnamese. I could see that he took me and my objectives seriously.

'Come and see the children,' I pleaded. A few days later he actually came to the centre with one of his colleagues. I shall never forget the sight of these two large men gently holding tiny fragile bodies in their arms. I could see they had tears in their eyes.

I was invited to lunch at the Enterprise office to meet the management team. I was excited, but terribly nervous. I felt I didn't have the right words to speak to these people, I didn't look professional. But this was a last-ditch stand. If Enterprise didn't back me, I had nowhere else to go. I could hardly swallow the curry and potato lunch, but as I got to my feet my doubts just left me, and I spoke to them as passionately as I had done to the grey-suited men in Hanoi.

A few days later Les gave me the verdict. Enterprise Oil would donate $10,000 to the new centre. I just threw my arms around this lovely man. 'I'll never let you down,' I kept saying. 'You'll never regret it.' I knew this was the beginning, the *real* beginning.

Enterprise were having their own offices built at the time and I asked Les Blair if I could talk to the builders. He introduced me to two local men, and I tried to explain my vision to them. I had to do it with my hands, because I'm no good at drawing.

'I want to keep it simple, I don't want anything big and foreign-looking, and in any case I don't have the money,' I said. 'I want it to look very light with a lot of fresh air going through, and windows down the side, here, and some steps at the front to walk up. I'd like a big area there where the children can have their sunbaths, and I want the toddlers to have little toilets, so they can sit down.'

Architects, builders, engineers and surveyors all came to

inspect the site. Gradually the plan for the Medical and Social Centre began to take shape. It was to be on three floors, with room for eighty-two children. On the ground floor there would be a special care unit to deal with acute problems. I wanted a teaching room where we could hold training seminars for staff and I also wanted an outpatients clinic. That was very important. The first floor would be for children who were recovering; and on the top floor there would be a day nursery to help poor parents who were at work.

We had to get the site properly surveyed, because there was water underneath it and we had to make sure the whole thing wouldn't sink into the ground. I was determined everything should be done properly, I didn't want it just thrown up. This building had got to work as a building and last for a very long time. Les Blair came to all the meetings but it seemed an awful responsibility. 'Jesus,' I kept thinking, 'the whole thing could collapse.' The team used to laugh at me, I was so nervous about it. 'It wouldn't kind of fall down, would it?' I asked several times.

We decided we'd have to demolish the dilapidated building we were taking over and start again. Long before the war it had been part of a convent and the government had taken it over from the sisters. I didn't know the building's history, I only knew that this was a place that had seen so much. In the middle of it there was a stone staircase, and there was something about that staircase. I thought of all the feet that had trodden it, and of what the building must have meant to people at various times. I didn't feel I had the right to demolish it completely, to destroy all those memories. I asked if we could incorporate the staircase into the new building, and that is what we did.

When everything was decided and I saw the estimates I was appalled. It was going to cost $60,000 – $50,000 more than

I had. For a while my natural optimism carried me along. God was good, I thought. Sure, didn't He build the whole world in six days and even have time to rest on the seventh. But reality soon struck home. I wasn't God. I was just plain old me, and I couldn't think of anyone who I hadn't already tried for money.

I looked across the compound at the dilapidated building and there seemed only one person left to appeal to. Passing the surly security guard, I went over to where there was a little room with an antiquated black telephone. It was so old it still had letters of the alphabet on the dial, and in my childish way I began to dial: H-E-A-V-E-N. I spoke into the telephone, which, appropriately for such a long-distance call, had slight interference on the line.

'Listen, God,' I said, 'I know you know everything that's going on. And you also know what point I'm at here. So where am I going to get the rest of the money from? You're going to have to be my consultant and guide me in all the right directions. Please, just tell me, how am I going to bring this off?'

And a voice in my head said, very clearly: 'One day at a time, Christina, one day at a time.'

'Okay,' I said. 'And I'm very grateful to you for the first handshake from Les Blair and Enterprise Oil. Goodnight now. I'll talk to you again tomorrow.'

I walked back across the compound to my room feeling better. Somehow my little charade had helped me to understand something important. Only if I took things step by step did I have a chance of winning. But I knew, and I felt God knew, that it was going to be a very long haul.

That night the monsoon rains fell heavily on Ho Chi Minh City. Next morning, half asleep, I put my feet on the floor and was surprised by a cushiony feeling. It was nice. I dug my feet

40

in deeper and they made a slight rustling sound. Jesus, I thought, I don't believe it. It's been raining dollar bills!

I opened my eyes properly and looked down. 'Oh my God,' I shrieked, 'what is this? I didn't ask for insects, I asked for dollars!' The whole floor was covered with a carpet of tiny black insects, millions and millions of them. I'd never seen anything like it.

I began to hop and jump like Jumping Jack Flash, screaming and swearing, trying to brush the insects off my feet. I shouted down to Lai, my Cambodian friend, who worked in the compound and who had been rescued by Vietnamese soldiers from the Killing Fields.

'Lai! Lai! Help me! There's millions of insects in here. I've been invaded!'

I heard Lai run quickly up the stone steps. She was laughing as she came into the room with a huge broom and began sweeping the insects away.

'Lai, has the end of the world come?' I said in bafflement.

'No, no, Mama Tina, sometime this happen. Same, same everywhere.'

I sat on the bed while Lai swept vigorously. But I almost choked when she suddenly asked me if I'd like an egg sandwich.

I looked down at the insects. 'No thanks, Lai. I think I've seen enough protein for one day.'

Lai just doubled up laughing.

Enterprise Oil gave me another $10,000, but there was still $40,000 to go. I took to frequenting the Floating Hotel. At that time the Floating Hotel, moored in the river, was the only real hotel in Saigon apart from the Rex, and it was the place where men always met for drinks to discuss business. I was so desperate I'd actually approach people and ask them if they could help.

Usually I got the brush-off, but one day I saw a man who somehow looked sympathetic. I was right. His name was Neil Rigden, a big Yorkshireman who was an independent oil company consultant in Vietnam. After hearing my story and visiting the orphanage compound with me, he agreed to give me $9,000. 'I don't know why,' he said, after I'd told him what I wanted to do, 'but I believe you.' It was a real boost to my sinking morale, but of course it still wasn't enough.

A few other foreigners were also getting to know me now – not as 'Mama Tina', as the street children did, but as a night-club singer. Singing is a necessity for me, in more ways than one. I've always sung from the time when I was a tiny girl. It unchains my heart and recharges my spirit. During these evening sessions at the clubs I'd comfort myself with the songs I loved. Songs from Ireland. Songs of love and romance. Sometimes even songs from another era and in another language, like Edith Piaf's '*Non, ne rien! Je ne regrette rien . . .*'. But the song I always sang then and still do is 'I Have a Dream'.

Then I'd say a few words about the children: 'I work for the children of Vietnam. We all have a duty to the children, to the poor. Please remember that the children need you.' And sometimes people would reach into their pockets.

It was now November 1990 and I was working with Madame Man. Talking with her at length one evening brought home to me another terrifying reality. I would have to fund the running of the new Centre, and costs for children and staff alone would be about $70,000 a year. And that figure didn't include the expensive medical equipment we were going to need.

I went back to my room and sat on my bed. Shivers ran down my spine as I absorbed the shock of what Madame Man had just made clear to me – $70,000, just to keep the Centre staffed and running! The building work had begun now, and there was definitely no turning back. But what had I started? How on earth could a nobody like me, with no credentials, raise that kind of money year after year . . . ?

Next day I was feeling feverish. My head ached and pounded and I kept vomiting. Bouts of shivering came and went, came and went, escalating into a high fever. I thought at the time that it was very serious flu, but I later discovered that it was malaria.

I didn't think much about the future during the next few days as I lay tossing and shivering on the bed. I was aware of Lai bringing a little statue of the Buddha into my room, and making an altar with candles. There was a cloudy, spicy perfume of burning joss-sticks, and in the back of my consciousness I could hear Lai's murmured praying: 'Mama sick, Mama get better.'

There came a point when I was sure that I was going to die, and I remember thinking, why had I had the dream? What would happen to my dream, and to the children? I began to speak to God, passionately, with all my soul, and suddenly I had the sensation of a great force reaching out to envelop me and a bright light shining. At that moment I thought: 'I'm dying. This is death.'

Then I found I had stopped shivering, and I lay there for some time in the semi-darkness. Finally, I got out of bed, very shaky, and went to the door. Lai was on the landing, and she looked at me as if I was a ghost, and exclaimed 'Mama!' My first thought was: 'Lai can see me. I must be alive.' She led me back to my bed, and for the first time in days I went quietly to sleep. When I woke up next morning I felt different – I wasn't an anxious little girl any longer. I knew what I had to do next. I had to get on a plane and go back to the UK to raise funds, and somehow tell people about the plight of the children in Vietnam.

I can't explain the experience, or my sudden decision. These intuitions were the only way I seemed able to work, and I suppose essentially it's what I still do today. I can't work within the norms, and I realize it makes life complicated for other people because there isn't always a clear, planned path ahead. It's difficult for me too. I try to work as other people do, but it's very alien to me.

I said goodbye to the children. Loc clung to me. Loc had a blind brother, Tue, who was four, and ten-year-old Loc spent most of his life carrying Tue around on his back. They were inseparable and the three of us had become very attached. I put my arms around them.

'Why you going away, Mama Tina?' Loc asked.

'I'm going to get you more money,' I said.

I prayed that what I was saying was true.

FIVE

I ARRIVED AT Heathrow jetlagged but determined. I couldn't wait to see my children, and went straight down to our little house in Woking. It had meant so much to us, that house. It was the first home the four of us had ever had together, the first place where we could live without the fear of violence and the terrible tension that that produced. By the time we were together again Helen, Androula and Nicolas were teenagers, and because it had always been us against Mario, I was a bit like one of them, just thrilled that we were able to live normally at last.

I hadn't even told the children I was coming, but they took it in their stride. We hugged one another as though we'd never let go, and within ten or fifteen minutes we were laughing uproariously. We'd always been so close. Over the years I had talked to them about Vietnam and the dream I'd had, and when I took my decision to go they had supported me a hundred per cent. They didn't seem to find it strange at all when I appeared unannounced and told them I wanted to build a children's clinic in Saigon.

Androula was studying sociology at university, Nicolas was

at sixth-form college, and Helen was already doing brilliantly with her career as a singer and songwriter. They were all fine, they reassured me. My heart was touched when I realized their main concern was for me.

It was strange waking up in suburban Surrey, with its neat silent houses and well-ordered gardens. I began to realize how much Vietnam had already entered my bloodstream – the energy of the Saigon streets and the nasal, high-pitched voices of the street vendors, the food carts with their mysterious smells. Life there was lived on the edge, but it was real.

There was no time to waste, so I took out the Yellow Pages and started making telephone calls to people I'd never spoken to before – journalists, businessmen, hospitals, anyone who would listen. It was a slow, discouraging process. The newspapers in England at that time were filled with stories of another tragedy, the fate of the children in Poland and Romania. People, I was told, were suffering from 'compassion fatigue' – a phrase that made me smile. Nobody wanted to hear about the children of Vietnam. That was all over.

But I suppose the story I was telling must have provided a new angle, because eventually it was taken up by Mary Riddell of the *Sunday People*. My life as an orphan and a street child, it seemed, hadn't been in vain. Mary's article was splashed right across the front of the paper. *This is the real Miss Saigon*, shouted the giant headline . . . *a legacy of war only one woman wanted to know*.

The response to this article was amazing. Money from the British public began pouring in, and I was interviewed by Frank Bough for Sky Television and on morning TV by Anne and Nick. I was beginning to understand the power of the media, and to see what fund-raising was all about.

I was invited to Ireland to appear as a guest on the *Late, Late Show*. Ireland. My stomach churned. The last time I'd seen

Ireland it had been from the deck of the old ferry we called the cattle boat on a wet and windy night when I was eighteen. I could feel all the losses hitting me again, Mam's death, the splitting up of the family, and the gaping hole they'd made in my heart when they'd taken my baby Thomas away from me. It wasn't only people I'd lost in Ireland. My body and my innocence had been stolen from me there too. Could I face those terrible memories? I asked myself the question, but I already knew I had to go.

I flew into Dublin on a soft, overcast day and was taken by car to Jury's Hotel, where the television company was putting me up. Me, I kept thinking, at Jury's – one of the poshest hotels in town. After I'd checked in I stood in my room, very still, looking at all the comfort around me. I'm not easily impressed, and in any other country, in any other hotel, these surroundings would have meant nothing to me. But this was Dublin. This was the city where I'd walked the streets from one endless day to another, staring at the lights in other people's houses, wishing I was one of them, inside, safe and secure. Dublin was desolation and despair to me, the place where I'd rummaged in dustbins in search of food, that had abandoned me to live like an animal in a hole in the ground.

Slowly I lay down on the bed and let my head sink into the mass of soft white pillows. I was taller now, stronger now, but simply being in this city made me feel emotionally reduced, raw and exposed, like a small child again.

I knew too that I was pushing back a grief that I didn't want to remember. My father's death in Birmingham a few months earlier had brought so much to the surface – the anger and the sadness I felt for his wasted, alcoholic life and what it had done to the rest of us. I had forgiven him, but I couldn't forget. Yet I also knew that it was these terrible memories that were enabling me to do the work that I had to do. We can live without an arm or a leg or an eye, I thought, but if we lose our memories, we don't know who we are, or where we have been, or where we are going.

I'd never been in front of an Irish audience before, and I was terribly nervous. The *Late, Late Show* in Ireland is the equivalent of the Michael Parkinson interviews in England or the Jay Leno show in America, and I knew thousands of people would be watching. When I arrived at the RTE studios the production team were very kind, but I was tense. When I heard the host of the show, Gay Byrne, introduce me I tried to smile and look confident as I stepped out into the glaring lights, but my heart was thundering, my knees were trembling, and my hands were clammy.

The vision of my mother's grave kept running through my mind, a pauper's unmarked grave in Mount Jerome cemetery where I'd seen her buried with strangers when I was only ten years old. And now here I was, a grown woman, back from the other side of the world and appearing on Irish television. But I didn't feel grown up. I felt lost, and unwelcome and unacceptable in that hot television studio. I had no reason to, but I did. My chest hurt and all the years of needing my mother and grieving for her seemed to hit me. 'Mammy,' I kept thinking, 'Mammy.' I wanted to cry, but instead I smiled to hide what was going on inside me. As they say, old habits die hard.

I could see that deep down Gay Byrne was a sensitive man, and I think he felt my distress. He drew me out very kindly and skilfully, and gradually I could feel myself beginning to relax. But it was the Irish studio audience who really made the day for me. As I told my story, they fell very quiet. I could tell that they were really listening, and I could *feel* this great wave of silent support. It turned what had started as a nightmare into a tremendous experience.

After that night, everywhere I went in Dublin people recognized me and treated me with the greatest kindness and love. It wasn't patronizing love either – it was genuine, and proud and sorrowful.

'If only I'd known you then,' one woman said to me, 'I'd have helped you, and fed you and loved you.'

But of course she couldn't have known me. I was like a frightened animal, hiding from a world that had abandoned me. I was nobody's child.

People gripped my hand tightly in the street, saying: 'God bless you, Christina, God love you.' I walked through the Liberties, and people still living in the Marrowbone Lane flats shouted to me across Henry Street, 'We saw you on the *Late, Late* last night, Ina! Jasus you were gorgeous. You looked like a movie star! God, we were proud of you.'

Their lovely, uninhibited Irish ways made me cry, and made me laugh. The Irish are by nature very generous and giving people, and now they were giving to me with their hearts and their hands. In the days after the show money flooded in from all over the country for the Centre and for the street children of Vietnam. One man in a café gave me £5 from his pension and it touched me deeply. Nothing could heal the pain of the past, but there was another healing beginning. It felt as if Ireland was giving something back to me that I had lost all those years ago.

Back in England I found that all my letters and phone calls were beginning to pay off there too. I spent more time calling on businesses, and visiting hospitals to ask for equipment they no longer needed. Androula and Nicolas and Helen did everything they could too, knocking on doors and organizing car boot sales. They had all the cheek I had. They went into wine shops and asked for wine to put in raffles, and grocery shops gave them food for hampers. It wasn't as if they were just doing something to help Mum, they were really buzzing with me. They were so wholehearted, and I was so proud.

By the time I flew back to Vietnam I had most of the medical equipment I needed. Following behind me in shipping crates were eleven incubators, forty new cots with special hot-weather mattresses, ECG machines, sterilizers, and enough medicines to keep us going for several months. But the greatest relief was that I'd raised enough money to finish the building work on the Centre, and to cover its running costs for the first year.

SIX

I RETURNED TO find work on the outside of the Centre almost finished. To everyone else it must have looked like any other simple, whitewashed, three-storey building, but in my mind's eye I could see the inside exactly as I'd dreamed about it. I wanted lots of colours – yellows, blues, reds, greens – and curtains with dolls on them, and Mickey Mouse and Donald Duck patterns . . . It would be warm and welcoming, and there would be toys, lots of toys.

Soon I realized how unrealistic these dreams were. Things like that simply weren't available in Ho Chi Minh City. When I talked about them the Vietnamese looked at me in disbelief. Why would I need these in a poor children's medical centre? 'You have no money,' people kept saying. It was true. For the time being I would have to make do with what I could get.

In any case, I realized, it was probably better to keep things simple and functional, Vietnamese-style. The eight toddlers' toilets had ended up looking very Vietnamese. I burst out laughing when I saw eight tiny round holes at ground level in a white-tiled surround. One thing, anyway, I was determined about. Everyone was going to understand that to me these were children like any other children. They were not 'dust of the earth' to me.

The Medical and Social Centre was officially opened on 1 June 1991 by Vice-Minister Quang. A large number of official people came, including my friend Mr Tue from the Ministry of Labour, Invalids and Social Affairs. The management from Enterprise Oil were there, and doctors and local dignitaries and people from the business community. The compound was packed.

Madame Man made a big deal of the opening. There was a wide red ribbon across the entrance, which Vice-Minister Quang and I cut together. Inside everyone sat on chairs while the Vice-Minister made a speech. Then Madame Man made a speech. They both spoke in Vietnamese so it was impossible for me to understand what they were saying but every few sentences, it seemed, I heard my name: 'Christina Noble . . . Christina Noble . . . Christina Noble.'

Then I had to say something. It was the first time in my life I'd made a speech and I was very frightened, but I did manage to thank the Minister, and the government and Madame Man for letting me do this, and Les Blair for believing in me. 'I know you'll be as proud as I'm feeling today,' I said. 'This is the beginning, please God, to find a new way for the children.'

Afterwards we all had cake and Vietnamese tea at tables with white sheets draped over them. Everyone was shaking my hand and I think I may have sung 'Danny Boy' or 'I Have a Dream'. I can't remember now. It all felt like a dream. The cots were in, we had a team of Vietnamese medical staff employed by Madame Man, and we were ready to open. I kept wondering how I'd done it. I still don't know. I wondered what my mother would have said to me if she'd been watching. Could she ever have believed her little tearaway would do something like this? I felt a combination of pride and a confidence I'd never felt before.

But the real fulfilment came when I saw the first mothers and children arriving. They came that same day, in a big rickety local bus with messy bits of pink curtain at the windows. They'd been sent by a local authority and they'd travelled a long way. I saw their faces at the window, just gazing at this new building, and then they looked at me standing on the steps.

They got down from the bus, looking shabby and very tired, and I held out my arms to them and said, 'It's okay now. It's okay.' If my arms had been big enough I'd have embraced them all, and I just kept thinking, 'Thank God. This is what it's really about.' I don't think I've ever felt so close to poor people as I did that day.

News of the Centre had appeared in the local papers and the word about it went round like wildfire. There's a very efficient bush telegraph among the poor. We were full with children immediately, many of them terrible, end-of-the-road cases of malnutrition. Some of them were already suffering permanent effects, children like little Le Le, who had lost both her parents within the first few months of her life.

Le Le was ten months old, and she came from the remote and very poor province of Ca Mau, in the heart of the Mekong Delta. After their parents died her fourteen-year-old brother had tried desperately to keep Le Le, hiding with her in a paddy field so that she wouldn't be taken away from him. They had nothing to eat, and eventually Le Le became so ill from lack of vitamins that she lost her sight. Her brother left her on the steps of a hospital, then ran away, obviously terrified that he would be blamed and punished for Le Le's condition.

Even now I often think about Le Le's brother and wish

desperately that I could tell him that none of it was his fault, that we know that he tried his best. I only hope one day he will find Le Le and won't have to live with the burden of his guilt and sadness any more.

Le Le was one of many children sent to the Centre from the remote provinces, but I've never seen a baby so withdrawn. She lay quite still in her dark world, her sunken face completely void of expression. When she did start to cry, there was no sound. Tears just rolled down her little face. Le Le had been completely traumatized by her experiences, and she needed all the love and affection we could give her to restore her will to live.

It was during the early days of the Centre that I first met another of our great little characters, Lap, who was to be part of our lives for a very long time. All the children are special to me, but Nguyen Tan Lap is a little boy very close to my soul. Lap was four when he and I first met, and it was love at first sight for both of us.

Lap's story of rejection is a typical one for disabled children in Vietnam. When he was a year old his mother had taken him to the paediatric hospital in District 2 to be treated for stomach pains, but she never came back to collect him. Nobody wanted Lap and he was transferred to the Centre for Malnourished Orphans. When Lap was almost two, he was adopted by a Vietnamese family. But within months it became clear that he was deaf and they brought him back.

When I first met Lap he used to follow me everywhere, trotting at my heels like a little Romeo. He couldn't hear my words or answer me, but his eyes understood a smile and his face knew what a kiss meant. We were always hugging and kissing, and Lap could read my moods better than most hearing children. I empathized with him in his silent world, and I loved his courage and determination and his ability to laugh. I wished I could do something more to ease his isolation, but at that point I simply didn't have the means.

The outpatients clinic was soon treating over a thousand children a month and I began to realize what a huge task we'd taken on. My weeks in the UK had left me drained, and the symptoms of malaria returned. There were difficulties, too, with some of the Vietnamese staff. I was often upset by the cold, impersonal way they handled and fed the children. Sometimes I had the feeling that they would have been much happier if I'd just provided the money and left them to run the Centre without me.

Often, after an exhausting day, I went back to my room and cried. But then I thought about the children. There was so much to be done, and change of any kind was bound to take time.

I had an old suitcase I carried round with me which I called my travelling office. Every receipt, every letter, every communication was thrown into it. Soon it was filled to overflowing, so I asked Madame Man if she would give me a bigger room. One of the compound workmen came up and put a board across it to divide it for me, and the front half became my new office. I had no office furniture or equipment, so most of my work was done sitting on the floor with pen and paper, using my old suitcase as a desk.

Our medical supplies were now running low. After the *Late, Late Show* in Ireland I'd met a kind man called Derek Shorthall. 'Just tell me what you need, Christina,' he'd said, 'and I'll see what I can do.' I took him at his word and faxed him a shopping list. It included everything from medicines and disposable syringes to potato crisps, Irish sausages and tins of mushy peas. I also asked if he could find us a paediatrician. Within a few days a reply came back: everything on the shopping list would be arriving, including the paediatrician.

Aideen Naughton, the paediatrician, was one of two volunteers who kept me going in those early days and did so
much to help cement relationships at the Centre. The other
was Joanna Pyner, a nurse from the East End of London.
During my rounds of hospitals in England I had met Joanna's
mother, who had not only given me the equipment I wanted
but had suggested contacting her daughter when I told her I
was looking for people with expertise.

Joanna inspired confidence as soon as she arrived. She was
very tall, with dark curly hair like Scarlet O'Hara in *Gone with
the Wind*, and a beautiful warm face. Nothing seemed to faze
her, though I could see she was a little shocked by my office.
At first we sat on the floor, using paper Joanna had brought
with her because I couldn't get supplies in Vietnam. After a
few days I went downstairs and scrounged a table from Lai, and
then I scrounged a chair. It wasn't suitable, I thought to myself,
to have professional people sitting on my hard, cold floor tiles,
getting a freezing bum and even the possibility of piles.

Joanna consulted with the Vietnamese staff and then, sitting
at the old table all day and sometimes half the night, she
working out a training programme. It was very professional,
with a blackboard and diagrams, and the staff loved it. Then
Aideen arrived, along with the bandages and the crisps and the
mushy peas, and she became part of the training programme
too. Everyone loved Aideen and Joanna, big time. Really big
time.

Aideen was tall, slim and beautiful, with light brown hair,
huge blue eyes and eyelashes like yard brushes. She had a
natural grace in dealing with people that allowed her to fit in
perfectly with the Vietnamese medical staff. As well as sharing
her paediatric knowledge, Aideen taught them about new
medicines and how to store them at the right temperature.
The antibiotic amphycillin had been widely used in Vietnam,

and this had resulted in a big immunity build-up. Now we had alternatives.

In the training programme Aideen and Joanna did the academic bit, the medical side, about saving lives, and important things like that. My bit was different. It was about love. I was terribly ignorant about Vietnamese culture at that time, but wherever you are, love is the same, it's a feeling from inside. So I stood up and talked about love.

Love is so important, I told the staff, and if we don't have love inside us to give, nothing Joanna or Dr Naughton are saying means anything. Children can cure themselves on love. It's the key that turns on the works, and it doesn't matter how you display it. The Vietnamese way is fine. But everyone needs to show love – it doesn't matter whether you're a mother, or a father, or a nurse, or a cleaner, or a cook, or a director.

Then I'd mime holding a baby in a loving, tender way. They understood.

At the same time I was venturing on teaching them English, because that was something they loved to learn. I'm not a teacher, but we had great fun.

'I – noun,' I'd say, 'want to dance and sing – verbs. A verb denotes action.' Then I'd do a dance and break into 'You ain't nothin' but a hound dog' and they'd be in stitches.

'I – want – to – sing,' they'd chant, roaring with laughter.

We laughed so much that eventually I wasn't really teaching them anything, it was more a pantomime, but it did help to break down the barriers.

Two of the staff, Dr Thanh and Chief Nurse Lam, I felt particularly close to. I could tell that they were people who cared very much about the poor and about children. They certainly didn't show it in the same way as I did, they were both very gentle and reserved. But I knew they wanted the Centre to succeed. Aideen worked beside Dr Thanh, and she told me she thought her a superb paediatrician and a superb human being. I knew that.

All this made me feel good. I had always wanted the Vietnamese to do their own thing. I'd never wanted to be a superior-seeming European coming in and telling them what to do. I saw myself as simply a tool that would help them turn the key and make things happen.

Although I knew so little about the country, I instinctively knew how not to tread on Vietnamese sensitivities. I think there's nothing worse than going into someone else's house and saying: 'Here, let me show you how to look after your child. Here, let me do the washing-up. Let me put this here and that there.' That is insulting. But it's all right to go into somebody else's house and say: 'Would you like me to hold the baby for you while you get on with the washing? Would you like me to get on with the washing while you do that? I've found a great new technique that works faster. Would you like me to show you?'

That was my attitude. Basically I was the run-around, and that is what I've continued to be, and I'm happy with it.

Aideen stayed for a while after Joanna had left, and the two of us would sit under the mosquito net at night, yapping into the small hours. I loved having Aideen there. And she never objected to the fact that supper was always egg and chips. It was all my budget would allow. I wanted to use every penny I could for the children. It was hard when she went. She had helped me during those evenings to laugh and to forget the pressures – the endless administrative tasks, the letter-writing and form-filling, the worries about the future.

When it all seemed too much, I'd think 'To hell with it!' and I'd run down and have a hug with the children to remind myself of the real reason I was in Vietnam. I've never cared what's wrong with a child, I'll cuddle them whether they have leprosy or TB. The feeling of being wanted is as important as any medical treatment.

> Nobody love me
> Nobody see me
> Nobody hear me
> Nobody care for me.
> You think me dirty
> You think me wild
> All you see is Nobody's Child.

That poem came from my heart. I knew I'd got to show the world that every one of these forgotten children was Somebody's Child. Somehow the world had got the blinkers on. People cared about the whales and the dolphins. But what good was all that, I thought, if they didn't care about the children?

Sunshine

SEVEN

So often, when I was talking to one of the street children, I'd hear the same thing. 'I wan' go school, Mama Tina.' They used to drag at me, saying over and over, 'Mama Tina, please help me. Help me study.'

It doesn't cost much to go to school in Vietnam, but for the street children it was impossible. Even the children who had parents were terribly poor, and the ones who were orphans, or who'd come from the provinces and got lost along the way, had no identities, so school was out of the question. Yet they knew as well as I did that they needed an education. How can you say no to a child who wants to go to school?

There was an unused shed in the compound, a concrete building with a corrugated iron roof, a bit smaller than a small English village hall, and the more I looked at it the more I was struck by its possibilities. I reckoned it would take about thirty-five children. I went to see Madame Man.

'Madame Man,' I said, 'can I use that shed for the children to go to school?'

Madame Man agreed it was a good idea. But there was a problem. A lot of these kids were supporting their families by working on the street all day and round the hotels, shoe-cleaning, selling Lotto tickets and souvenirs. I'd done it myself to help keep my brothers and sisters, selling shamrocks on the streets of Dublin. They were often working till four or five in the morning, when the shadowy figures of the adults would be waiting behind cars and in doorways to pick them up. It was going to be difficult for them to go to school. But I felt there must be a way. Perhaps we could make school hours flexible, I thought, maybe only two or three hours a day. At least they could learn to read and write and do arithmetic.

So Madame Man agreed to find some teachers, and for $60 I got the shed smartened up and painted yellow inside – sunshine yellow. I got a blackboard, and some little benches with desks that opened. I wanted the children to have proper-looking desks, with places inside for their books. We supplied everything they needed, schoolbags, pencils, pens, textbooks, jotters. We decided to call it the Sunshine School.

The day the school opened was superb. So many children turned up, we just didn't know what to do with them. They were sitting behind the desks, on the floor, spilling out into the compound, little kids in scruffy clothes, some of them with no arms, sitting in school for the first time. They all had their new schoolbags, and I saw one of the little guys with only one arm putting his ruler in and out, in and out.

First of all the children made speeches about why they wanted to go to school.

'If we no go school we no get jobs,' one of them said. 'My country now, many change, but we no get job. Now we go school we learn everything, reading, writing, mathematic. Then we get good job. Number One.'

Most of the girls wanted to work in offices. 'I want to work offich. In offich very nice. Wear glasses. Do like this,' they'd say, pretending to type.

Others had their own ideas. One little girl wanted to go to university. A boy wanted to study electronics. Another tiny child said he wanted to be able to read the newspaper.

The Social Affairs Department had come, and so had the police, and the police served lunch and waited on the children. Altogether it was a wonderful day and the kids were over the moon.

Classes were in the early morning, before the tourists were about, before the business of the day really started. It was cool then too. Later on, the shed with its corrugated iron roof was stifling. The children were as keen as mustard. What a contrast to the sad, bored children I'd often seen in the West. These kids really wanted to learn. When tourists asked them if they went to school, they'd puff up with pride. 'Shoor, oh shooor,' I heard one of them say, imitating the American accent. 'Me go Mama Tina *Shunshine* School. Number One school. You wan' see Mama Tina? I bring you.'

Sometimes the kids really would bring tourists to our office. 'Mama Tina, me bring lady and man from America. Many monies. I ask them give monies to Shunshine School,' they'd whisper. 'Me say Mama Tina very good, number one, no problem. But I say Mama Tina *very* tired. Little monies.'

Then they'd give me a big grin. 'Mama Tina, they give you many monies! My birthday nex' week. I like some shoe, okay?'

Unfortunately, the tourists the children brought were usually anything but rich. Mostly they were backpackers, students on very low budgets, who'd give us their small change when they were leaving Vietnam. It was usually just a few dollars, but the children thought we were getting a fortune.

Today our education programme is one of the Foundation's big success stories, but at that point, all I could think of was how I was going to find the money to keep the school open. I needed about $20,000 a year. I felt permanently anxious.

Every time I made a phone call I wondered if I'd be able to pay the phone bill. At night I slept fitfully, tossing and turning, and waking at dawn.

I developed the habit that I still have of getting up and cycling down to the market area around five in the morning, looking for children who were sick and in real distress. In the cool of the morning, dressed in my loose cotton trousers and loose cotton top, I'd walk through the narrow alleys where I knew I'd find children who'd been sleeping rough and alone.

One morning on my rounds I came across Mai. She looked about seven, but I found out later that she was ten. She knew who I was and we had a little chat – or rather I did. Mai said very little. She seemed completely lost. I asked her if she'd like a drink, and we went to a café.

Mai looked very neglected. She was terribly thin and her shoulder-length black hair was dull and dry. I noticed that the skin was peeling off her fingers, and her face and arms were covered in mosquito bites which had become infected from scratching. When we'd both finished our drinks I asked if she wanted to come and see me at the Centre and gave her my card. She nodded, but she seemed far away, and somehow I thought I wouldn't see Mai again. But to my surprise she did come, later that morning.

Through an interpreter Mai told us her story. It was familiar. Her mother and father, she said, used to have big fights, and then her father threw her mother and her little brother out, but he made Mai stay. Then her father brought a new girl-friend home, and six months later he threw Mai out on to the streets too.

'How long have you been living on the streets?' I asked. 'Two Tets,' she said. The annual New Year Tet celebrations were the only way the little girl could measure time. I could see that she was very frightened. She told us that men had come up to her, asking if she would like to go abroad. She'd heard that children could be kidnapped on the streets and sent to foreign countries where they were made to do bad things, and this terrified her.

She was obviously exhausted, so I lifted her feet up on to the wooden bench, put a pillow under her head and a teddy bear in her arms that was almost as big as she was, and gave her a big kiss. She was already asleep and she didn't wake up until two o'clock. When I saw her again she was clinging on to the teddy bear as she tucked into a plate of rice and vegetables, and she seemed less frightened.

I found some old children's frocks for her to dress the teddy and an old scarf which I tied round its head. For the first time I saw Mai smile. We talked to one another again through an interpreter.

'Mai, do you have any dreams?' I asked her. She didn't answer, just kept playing with the teddy, but after about five minutes she said, 'I have three dreams.'

Her first dream, she told me, was to find her mother and her brother. She started to sob, and I lifted her on to my lap and cradled her. Gradually her sobs subsided so I asked her, 'Do you ever have any children's dreams, like I did when I was small?'

She looked puzzled, so I told her how I'd dreamed of a yellow house, with everything in it yellow like sunshine. And I told her that once I'd even dreamed of going to the moon on the back of a fox.

This tickled Mai, and she said to the social worker who was with us, looking at me under her eyelashes, 'But I think Mama Tina too big to go on fox.'

'I was small and skinny like you when I went on the fox,' I explained. 'But if I went to the moon now I'd have to go on a buffalo.'

This really cracked Mai up, and she started laughing and laughing until she nearly fell off my knee. I could see she felt safe now, and she told us that she dreamed of having a pink dress with red roses and a long red sash. She also dreamed – as I know *all* Vietnamese children dream – of having her own bicycle.

It would be pink, and it would have butterflies on it that would shine in the dark.

Never make fun of a child's dreams, I always tell people. However poor and scruffy they are, children always have a dream. Sometimes it's all they do have.

'Oh,' I said, 'those are beautiful dreams, Mai. Beautiful, beautiful dreams. I can't promise, but I'll try very hard to make them come true. I may not be able to manage all of them.' I was determined, however, to try to find Mai's mother.

There were so many vulnerable children abandoned on the streets. I knew that they needed a place of shelter where they could perhaps be united with their parents, or where they could stay and go to school and gradually be accepted back into the community. But at present that was just a pipe-dream. There weren't enough hours in the day to do what I had to do already. And everything took money.

By now I'd sold everything I had to sell, including my jew-ellery, and I had lost my little house in Woking. It had been a bitter blow. One evening, in utter despair, I phoned Les Blair, and when I heard his friendly voice I started crying.

'I've got no money left, Les,' I said. 'And I mean *no* money.'

Les could hear the panic in my voice. 'I'll see what I can do,' he said, and next day he guaranteed me enough money to keep going for another month. During the next few weeks I put a brave face on it, but I felt bleak.

At this time I was still bashing away in my office on the old-fashioned typewriter, writing letters and filling in endless forms, helped by a young Vietnamese volunteer called Annie.

We had one little book and in it Annie wrote down all the Centre's incomings and outgoings. Every single dime we received and spent was recorded in it, and Annie was very scrupulous.

Mostly, however, Annie daydreamed about going to live in America. Like Lai she was a dedicated Buddhist, but at that time I had no idea what Buddhism was. 'You Buddha, Mama Buddha,' Lai would sometimes say to me, which made me laugh. She could have been calling me a dipstick for all I knew. Annie, whose English was better, explained the idea of reincarnation to me and I made a joke of it. 'What do you reckon I'll come back as?' I said. 'Jaysus, I'd like to come back as a gekko. Then I can catch mosquitoes.' They used to laugh their hearts out.

One day, when I was feeling particularly tired and ill, Lai came and stood beside me. She began to bow. 'Mama sick,' she said. 'Lai speak Buddha, help Mama. Mama Buddha, same same Buddha. No same everybody.' She was speaking with great reverence, and then she began to cry. 'Lai love Mama,' she kept saying. 'Same same Buddha.'

Knowing very little about Buddha, I wasn't sure what Lai was saying. I only knew it was serious. I was very respectful about Buddhism after that, and at that bleak time I felt especially warmed by Lai's affection.

Another person who was to be a great support to me joined the Centre that year, Helen Thuong, who is now our Vice-Director. Unusually, I had gone to the pool one afternoon and, standing awkwardly on the edge, I fell into conversation with a Frenchwoman who was a film-maker. The result was the first film ever to be made about the Centre, *Enfant de Personne* or *Nobody's Child*. During filming the sound engineer, who had been born in Cambodia, introduced me to his aunt. This was Helen.

Like so many Vietnamese Helen had lost everything after the war, suffering terrible hardships, and she needed a job. She was very tiny and thin and her voice was only a whisper.

'I've no money to pay you,' I said sadly.

'That is all right,' she said. 'I will work for nothing. One day maybe you will be able to pay me.'

So Helen came to work for us for $10 a month, and gradually her pay crept up to $20, then $30, then $40, then $50. Helen has great inner strength and a quiet, concentrated way of being, and she loves children. Soon I couldn't imagine the Centre without her. Madame Man had become increasingly busy with work for the government in other parts of Vietnam. But now I had Helen to help me. And an office with a table and a chair. Things were coming on.

We were also getting used to visits from media people. A journalist and photographer called Gail Fisher produced a feature that ran across two full pages of the *Los Angeles Times*. I was pictured with one of the children who had no arms or legs. I was incensed by the plight of the children and by what had happened to Vietnam, and I didn't mince my words. Then an American television company arrived to make a film, and before long I was being invited to appear on TV in America.

I was so busy that I had no time to prepare for my trip. I arrived in New York without even a pair of decent shoes, and had to borrow some for my appearance on a breakfast-time slot called the *Home Show*. I was just packing my bags again when the phone in my hotel room rang.

'This is the William Morris Literary Agency,' said the voice. 'Could you come in and see us? We think you've got a great story.'

'I can't,' I said. 'I'm flying to Canada tomorrow to talk to a school, and then I'm going back to Vietnam.'

'To a school?' The voice sounded incredulous. 'Couldn't you cancel that?'

'No,' I said, 'I can't. I've promised, and the children will be disappointed.'

So the man from William Morris flew to Toronto to meet me. Within days I was back in New York signing a book contract. While I was sitting in his office the agent disappeared. 'There's a German publisher outside who'd like to meet you,' he said when he came back. 'Tell him your life story. You'll have to be quick, he's only got three minutes.'

I was in another world, I realized, where experiences could be reduced to a matter of dollars and Deutschmarks. I didn't like the feeling of it, I didn't like it at all. But I reasoned that a book would give me a platform to campaign for children across the world, and it could also raise funds for the Centre. So I managed to say a few words and the German rights to my book were snapped up by Hans Peters of Heyne Verlag. I had no idea, then, how much all this would change my life, or what a painful inner journey I would be making.

EIGHT

A FEW MONTHS later I flew to Atlanta to meet Robert Coram, who was to collaborate with me on my book. The first few days were difficult for both of us. I think Robert, who at first sight looked like a typically tough American journalist, must have wondered what he'd taken on. I had fooled myself into thinking I could produce a book without delving too deeply into the parts of my life I didn't want to remember. I could almost hear Robert thinking to himself, 'Shit, man. Who is this Irish woman they've sent me?'

We sat together on the terrace of Robert's comfortable house in the Atlanta suburbs. Robert is a real professional, and gradually he got me talking about myself. We began to like one another. My story moved and disturbed him. But I knew there was a lot I was holding back, and so did he.

'I think we should go to Ireland,' he said, so together we flew to Dublin. But I didn't want to relive it all again. I was trying to avoid talking about the sexual abuse I'd suffered, the rape when I was sixteen. I didn't want to walk back down the streets where I'd felt such desolation. I didn't want to visit my mother's grave, or the mortuary where she had been laid. I didn't want to talk about Thomas's birth and how I felt when he was taken away. These things were too painful to put into words.

Suddenly I couldn't take Robert's questions any more. 'Don't keep asking me these terrible things,' I sobbed. 'Don't you understand, it's killing me. I can't do this book.' The sobbing was coming from deep down, shaking my whole body. I felt vulnerable and lost, like a small child. But I was angry too as I sobbed my heart out. It was a catharsis of a kind.

Robert was very calm. 'Look,' he said, 'I'm going to stop right here. We'll start again in the morning, and either we do the book or we don't.' I knew he was right. Next morning I began to talk more openly. Together we walked through the Liberties and along the Dublin quays where I'd been forced into a car before I was raped. 'I saw you totally change,' Robert said that evening. 'You had your head down, and you stuck your hands in your pockets. You rounded your shoulders and walked close to the wall. I saw a little girl walking down there, not you.'

Then we took a car and drove to Connemara. That was one of the most horribly vivid memories of all. As we rounded the last corner and saw the building, I was right back in the autumn of 1957 again, arriving like a criminal, under police escort.

The black police car drove slowly past the front of St Joseph's Convent, which was all flowers and rockery and greenery, and turned slowly right over a cattle grid, through black iron gates, and round to the Industrial School at the rear.

St Joseph's Industrial School in Clifden, Connemara. This was the second institution I'd been sent to. I had escaped from the first and I'd been living on the Dublin streets for a year and a half, sleeping in Phoenix Park. Connemara was the end of the world to me, so far out west. I felt like an exile, banished for some dire crime I had not committed.

I wanted to cry, but I knew I mustn't. If they thought me a softie, the other kids would get me. 'Well,' I kept telling myself, 'I can always run away. It's fifty miles to Galway, and from there I can follow the tracks right back to Dublin.'

A nun opened the door. The two female police escorts who had travelled in the car with me handed her a legal document. 'Christina Byrne, Sister. You'll find all her details in there.'

I stepped inside on to the cold red-tiled floor and heard the door bang behind me. The nun didn't look directly at me. A large pair of black rosary beads hung down to her thighs and at her side was a long thick cane with reeds on the end. I could see she was a vexed type of nun, and I was afraid.

A little woman came into the hall and stood in front of the nun. She wore an old apron over her cardigan, and her frock hung down to her shin-bones. Thick brown stockings, wrinkled like steps, mounted up her little short legs above her brown-laced shoes. Mary Early.

Mary had been brought to St Joseph's as a small baby and this was the place she was going to die in. She was a real old battleaxe, but sometimes I felt a kind of pity for her. She had a tiny crinkled face, with thick-glassed spectacles sitting on the bridge of her nose, and her eyes were like grey marbles rolling around as she inspected me. A big bunch of keys jangled in her hand. She looked like my jailer.

They went abruptly into a side room. 'Watch this one, Me-e-ery!' I heard the nun, Sister Philomena, say. 'She'll try to escape. So keep a close watch on her. She's wild.'

Without looking at me Mary Early said, 'Follow me.' She was almost running in front of me, shuffling her flat feet on the floor and dangling her powerful keys. I followed her into

74

a room with cold white tiles on the wall. It could have been a fridge I was in.

'Now take off your clothes,' she said indifferently. I remember thinking, 'I hope she goes outside.' I didn't want her to see my knickers which were grey-looking and held up with a big safety-pin.

'All of them,' she said, as I fumbled. Minutes later I stood before her naked. I felt dirty and ashamed as she rolled her grey marble eyes around my body. With a red pencil she made several partings in my hair, checking for lice. She looked at my feet. Her cold eyes pierced my tiny budding breasts.

'Hold your arms up,' she ordered. She checked under my arms and between my legs.

I was shivering with a combination of cold and fear, and I dug my nails hard and painfully into my palms. Was she going to examine me? Would she know that the man we stayed with had done dirty things to me?

The door opened sharply, and the woman I nicknamed 'Rubberbelly' came in. She had a big stick, like the leg of a chair, in her hand. She cast a cold, uninterested eye over my body, then took me to another room where there was an enormous bath with giant taps. It was full of brown water with steam swirling above it.

Rubberbelly put some liquid from a bottle into the water. 'Get in,' she said. The water was scalding. She scrubbed me with a hard scrubbing brush until some parts of my body bled. She scrubbed my hair until the scalp almost lifted off my head. I sat with my shoulders hunched, trying to cover my breasts, and my silent tears fell into the disinfected water.

When she was finished she handed me a long flannel shift to put on. It was so big I could have put all my brothers and sisters in it. Then she cut off all my hair, tight to my skull.

Mam, Mam! Mam used to like to put rags in my hair, tiny

bunches at a time, so that it would fall into curls, ready for when I would go on stage and tap dance. Mam wouldn't have liked what they were doing to me. I knew Mam couldn't help me because she was dead, yet I still couldn't really believe it. Rubberbelly poked her stick into my back and told me to sweep up the hair on the floor. 'Follow me,' she ordered when I had finished.

Laid out on a table in another room was a pair of heavy black-laced brogues, one pair of thick knitted black stockings and one pair of white socks, and a navy gymslip and a navy skirt that hung down to my calves. There were also two strips of thick white flannel that were to be used as sanitary towels month after month. I could see from the washed grey look of them that they had been used before.

Finally I was handed two ugly rusty-red knitted jumpers with the number 69 stitched on the back. This was my new identity, a child prisoner, incarcerated among the ranks of the soldiers of God.

God. If these so-called Brides of Christ understood God as I did, how could they have these bitter faces and cruel hearts? St Joseph's Industrial School wasn't so much a school as a slave labour camp, where the illegitimate were seen only as the products of mortal sin, and the poor and legitimate, like me, as merely contemptible.

You spoke only when you were spoken to. Breakfast was two pieces of bread with a scrape of butter in the centre. Dinner was sick-lamb and potatoes, smothered with gravy made from flour and the fat scooped off the side of the pot. I knew the lambs were sick because I used to have to clean the maggots off them in the dairy. If visitors brought tins of sweets or biscuits for us children, the nuns took them over to the convent and gave them to their colleagues, the Sisters of Mercy.

At night, when we crawled under the grey blankets of our

iron beds, the last thing we'd see before the lights went out was Rubberbelly with her stick.

'*Turn!*' We'd all turn to the right. '*Face press! Lights out!*' Pitch blackness.

Then I sobbed – for my dead Mammy, and my useless drunken Daddy, and my brothers and sisters, and our life in the Liberties that was now over. Were Sean and Philomena and Kathy as unhappy as I was? I didn't even know where they were. Perhaps if I wrote, someone in Dublin would know. I asked one of the nuns for some paper. When I told her what it was for she said to me coldly, 'You don't have a family. They're dead.'

I later discovered that this is what my brothers and sisters had been told too, even my little brother Sean, who I used to call Johnny. When he escaped from the Christian Brothers' notorious school at Letterfrack and came in search of me, they just told him I was dead and sent him back.

Sister Philomena was determined to beat the spirit out of me. If she ever caught me singing or dancing she'd take me into the room beside the kitchen and lay about me with the cane. But there was nothing that could stop me singing. It was my release and my consolation.

There was a girl who worked over in the convent, I think she was called Imelda, and when she was carrying the food left over by the nuns in a bucket down to the pigs she had to pass our building. A crowd of us used to run out and raid the bucket and eat what we had grabbed. The pigs never got a look-in.

One day Imelda told me a roadshow was coming to town. There was going to be a talent competition. She suggested I should ask Sister Philomena if I could sing in it.

When I asked Sister Philomena she looked at me as if I had

committed a mortal sin. Her stare was enough to make me say 'Sorry, Sister,' and walk away.

I thought about it for days, and then I went to see Marie Green. Marie was a gentle girl who played the piano beautifully with her long, slim fingers. Her hair was tied back with a nice green ribbon and her shoes were always polished. The nuns loved her because she was a good girl, and she was allowed to wear a *green* cardigan, instead of the institutional navy. Sister Bernadette, the music teacher, really liked her. We all did. Marie had a soul for music, a real soul.

'Marie,' I said, 'if you could see your way to telling Sister Bernadette that I'd like to sing in the contest and *you* would like to play the piano for me, then Sister Bernadette could ask Sister Philomena, and I think she'd agree. Think about it, Marie. You don't know who might be out there listening and pick up on your talent! Sometimes you get people coming all the way from America. Talent spotters.'

Marie was not an impulsive type. She looked at me. She could see I was really serious. 'Well,' she said finally, 'I don't know if they'll listen to me, but I'll try.' She came back to tell me they had agreed – on condition that I sang a song that they would choose for me.

In the Music Room Sister Bernadette had me standing up straight, feet together, hands clasped, held between my breastbone and the upper part of my stomach.

The song they'd chosen was a slow, high-pitched song, a bit like you'd sing in church.

> In Conn-e-mara by the lake
> Tw-oo young hearts had to break
> In Co-ounty Galway by the sea
> Where I met you-ooo
> And you-ooo met me . . .

They'd taken out the word 'loved' and put in 'met'.

On the big day I went down to the town in a borrowed frock and cardigan. I think the frock was a Mary Early cast-off. My hair was in a plain hairband. I looked like Miss Jean Brodie.

The marquee was packed and the sun was shining. There was a good atmosphere, all the people from the villages had come to the show. There was all sorts of selling going on: cattle and horses, cake-stalls, balloons. Cabbages and flowers were being judged.

Marie had been allowed to bring me into town and we showed our passes to the man at the marquee entrance. Inside I looked straight ahead of me at the stage. Oh God, it reminded me of old times! It was decorated beautifully. Huge drapes of shiny coloured paper shimmered in the background. A band was playing 'Red River Valley'.

My body started to jig automatically. 'Oh, I love it, Marie. I love it. Do you feel great, Marie, do you feel great?'

Marie looked at me. 'Now you promise me that you'll sing that song. "Connemara by the lake" . . .'

'Of course I will.'

'Do you promise me?'

'Yes.'

There were a few more acts before us – Irish dancers in beautiful emerald green dresses and boys with short trousers and black brogues, and grey knee-socks with little bits of green sticking out the sides.

Oh, the sounds were wonderful. I couldn't wait for our turn. I just couldn't wait. I wished I was wearing a shimmering lilac top hat and tails, with a white cane and nice white buckskin boots with jingle taps. I hated the clothes I was wearing. I decided to imagine I *was* dressed in a lilac top hat and tails. That's how I'd go out on stage.

79

'Ladies and gentlemen, Christina Byrne and Marie Green are here to perform for you. Christina will sing and Marie will play the piano.'

Oh, the adrenalin started to flow. We mounted the steps. I stood in front of the microphone and Marie played a beautiful introduction, ending with the chords of 'Where I met you-ooo and you-ooo met me'.

Marie looked across the piano, her eyes met mine, and in that moment I knew she knew what was going to happen.

I burst into 'Stupid Cupid, you're a real mean guy! I could clip your wings so you can't fly . . .'

Marie went white. After a few seconds she just played some fast chords. I was shaking and rocking and rolling as I sang. The place was in an uproar, bird-whistles, clapping, cat-calls.

I sang more songs, tap-dancing across the stage. 'Zippedeedoodah, zippedeeday, my oh my, what a wonderful day . . .' I lifted my imaginary lilac top hat and waved it above my head.

Everyone was clapping and shouting 'More, more!' I sang another song and finished with a slow walk off the stage, shaking my hand to the rhythm and the audience – 'You got me singing the Blues . . .'

A quick twirl and my leg kicked high in the air, 'Yeahhhhh!'

Marie looked like a ghost as she came off stage. 'The nuns are down there!' she whispered. I peeped through the curtain. There they were, Sister Bernadette and Sister Philomena, marching towards the stage, their hands folded inside their black sleeves. Sister Philomena's face, purple as a beetroot, told me everything.

Back at St Joseph's Marie got a telling off, but no beating. The nuns knew it wasn't her fault.

I was marched into the room off the kitchen. Sister Philomena had a field-day with her cane and her mouth. My head was shaved again, and from that day on she beat me at every opportunity.

But I never regretted doing it. It was the best few hours I'd had for a very long time. And one day, I knew, I was going to escape, and be free and sing in America like Doris Day.

So now, nearly forty years later, I'd been to America. I was full of hope, after Gail Fisher's article and my appearances there, that once my work was known I'd be able to raise millions. God knows why. But I had never been to the United States before and I was still very naïve. I thought the film ABC television had made would attract donations, but none flowed in after it was shown. Nobody, I was told, had known where to send the money.

After that visit, some of the scales began to fall from my eyes. The Vietnam War had scarred America. The US government was still operating its crippling humanitarian and trade embargo, and though the war was over an emotional war was still going on. The appalling long-term effects of Agent Orange were still relatively unknown. Vietnam was an embarrassment.

NINE

My autobiography was published in Germany, in 1992, under the title *Niemanskind, Nobody's Child*. To publicize the book I flew to Munich, then on to Berlin, Cologne, Frankfurt, Düsseldorf, Hamburg. I appeared on television and I was interviewed by newspapers and magazines. One strange bedroom began to look very much like another as I unpacked my bags and tried to snatch a few minutes' break before I was collected for yet another publicity event. I found it all exhausting.

But as soon as I was in front of an audience, something – or Someone – would take over and the words would come pouring out of me. 'I work for the children of Vietnam . . .' I spoke from my heart. I knew I still needed to raise money to cover the running costs of the Centre for another year and I hoped that this tour, and the sales of the book, were going to solve my financial problems.

I was also realizing that an office in Vietnam wasn't enough. Local businesses alone couldn't support us. I needed some kind of international network if I was going to be able to carry on. My German publishers, Heyne Verlag, were enthusiastic about the book, and also very kind. Hans Peters suggested that they help me set up a registered office in Germany, a legal address to which people could send funds. With Les Blair's help we had already done this in London, and I accepted gratefully.

There was news that upset me back at Tu Xuong Street. Lap had been transferred to another children's centre while I was away. He was seven now, and Madame Man and the rest of the staff felt it was time for him to be with children of his own age. I was aware that because of his deafness Lap needed special help and I worried about how we could give it to him. But I couldn't bear the thought of him in a big institution. We were his family, his pals now, and Lap was such a free spirit, I knew he wouldn't be happy. I told Madame Man I wanted him brought back.

We were still looking for Mai's mother. It is very difficult to find children's parents in Vietnam, and it is mostly done by word of mouth. You put it around among the street people, and it travels like a bush telegraph. Mai was much less frightened now, but she was pining for her mother and her little brother. I took her down to Phu Ben Ten Market one evening and we spoke to a young girl called Phung who had once lived on the streets. Word came back through Phung that Mai's mother had been seen sleeping on the street in Pham Ngu Lao. It wasn't Mai's mother, but in time we did locate her, and one of our Vietnamese social workers went to talk to her. I knew that if I went it would cause too much loss of face. These situations are sensitive, and I had learned to step back.

The Centre itself was packed to overflowing. Families were bringing sick and malnourished children to us from the provinces, travelling two or three hundred miles. Many of these parents looked exhausted and starved, and I'd go out with them and buy rice and bags of dried fish or beef for them to take away – I just couldn't send them off empty-handed.

I was exhausted myself. The strain of the book and the tour was beginning to tell. Every time I got up on stage I was reliving a childhood I'd spent a lifetime trying to undo. I was desperate for these polite Western audiences to hear the voice of abandoned children, and I poured out my soul. But every time I did it I paid a price.

On the advice of a doctor I moved to a small apartment. It cost $400 a month, which left me $400 a month to live on from the small salary I was paid, but I knew the doctor was right. I had to get away, even if it was only for a few hours a day. Sometimes I'd still go downtown and sing my troubles out in front of the nightclub audience at one of the big new Western-style hotels.

I'd heard a rumour that one of these, the Saigon Star, was serving real cauliflower cheese. For me there is absolutely nothing to beat a plate of grilled cauliflower cheese with some sizzling Irish sausages and a nice cup of tea, so my Vietnamese friend Johnjo invited me to come and investigate.

Johnjo was always full of plans. We'd nicknamed him 'Mr Coffin' because he dreamed of having his own coffin business. He had worked out that the stress of doing business in Vietnam was likely to induce heart attacks in plenty of expat business-men and his idea was to open an office at the airport. There he would welcome them personally, explain the risks, and suggest that they might like to consider placing an order with him – just in case – for an expatriate-style coffin, with a choice of woods and a silk or satin lining. If desired, Johnjo could even arrange for the coffin to be draped in the appropriate national flag when it was shipped back home. It was an enterprising idea, but unfortunately Johnjo had overestimated the market.

We sat in the Saigon Star's breezy rooftop restaurant. My mouth started watering when a waiter with a white starched napkin over his arm made his way towards our table. Already I could taste the creamy florets with their grilled yellow cheese coating . . .

Soon the waiter reappeared with a domed silver cover. Beneath it was a white porridge bowl, which he plonked in front of me. In it was something grey and lumpy – a piece of cauliflower sitting in a pool of water, with a sparse sprinkling of what looked like soap powder on top.

Oh, the disappointment! Johnjo was already tucking into the ham sandwich he'd ordered, which he'd plastered liberally with mustard. It made me feel even hungrier.

'What's this?' I said to the waiter. 'I asked for cauliflower cheese.'

'Yes, Madam. This is cauliflower cheese.'

'Oh, go away with you,' I said.

'Yes, Madam,' and he walked away.

After a while I called him back. 'This cauliflower cheese is not cauliflower cheese,' I said, 'so I'd like to see the manager.'

A few minutes later a man in his early thirties, dressed smartly in a black suit, approached.

'I am the assistant manager,' he said politely, 'you asked to see me?'

'Yes,' I said. 'I must tell you this is not cauliflower cheese. Look at it – it's just a malignant growth drowning in dishwater.'

He looked at me, very cool, calm and polite. 'Yes, I'm sorry. Our normal chef is off today, so I think that is where the problem lies. Would you like to choose something else?'

'No,' I said, 'because if the chef is off then the rest of the food is probably off too. I'm definitely not paying for this load of old mush. But I'll tell you what, we'll have two cups of coffee and don't charge us for them.'

Against his will the assistant manager smiled. 'That's not a problem.'

I liked his politeness. We began to talk. I told him about my work, and he was obviously impressed that I, a foreigner, should care so much about the children of Vietnam. I learned that his name was Dan, which in Vietnam is pronounced 'Young'.

Later we went for a coffee, and talked about the problems of foreign tourism and the street children. Eventually Dan said, 'I would like to do whatever I can to help you.'

'Well, then,' I said, half-laughing, 'why don't you come and work with us?'

He half-smiled. 'Maybe.'

Dan began helping at the Centre as a volunteer, and three months later he resigned his job and joined us. It was a courageous step, because jobs don't come easily in Vietnam. Today he is our Assistant Manager and I can trust him to manage any situation. He speaks four languages and communicates with our associates abroad, meets Vietnamese government officials to discuss our work and travels to the provinces to check on our projects.

So inviting me to the Saigon Star for cauliflower cheese was one of Johnjo's ideas that *did* pay off.

TEN

Early in 1993 I got a call from an Australian journalist, Leigh Hatcher, who'd heard about my work. Leigh asked if he could come and maybe make a short film about the Centre. I remember hesitating, but as soon as I met him I had no doubts. Leigh is a family man and a person of great spirituality. He's also a brilliant film-maker and he managed to shoot a beautiful film in only a couple of hours.

When Leigh's film was shown in Australia the television audience loved it. A woman called Lois Jones telephoned to tell me how moved she had been and to suggest she arrange a promotional tour for me. Within two weeks, accompanied by Dan, I was on a plane to Sydney. I shall always thank God for sending Leigh Hatcher because he opened the door to Australia for me. Indirectly, he also saved my life.

I loved Australia from the moment I landed. People seemed so open-hearted. Lois Jones and her husband Lloyd had invited us to stay in their home in a comfortable area of Sydney and Lois had done a great job in preparation for my tour. A red helicopter arrived to fly me to an interview with Channel 7 in Sydney and I was stunned by the view of the

Opera House and the city spread out beneath me around the bay.

This time I was more confident and, as in Ireland, the sympathy I felt from the studio audience somehow held me. Phone calls poured in, and I was asked to appear on the show again later in the same week. Secretly, however, I wasn't feeling well. I was often dizzy and twice I fainted, but I kept telling myself it was just worry. I was doing too much.

Later that week in the Green Room at the TV studios a man approached me and introduced himself. His name was John D'Arcy, and he was a doctor with a regular programme on Channel 7.

'I think you should have a health check-up,' he said. I flannelled a bit, but he said to me, very seriously, 'Don't leave it. Have one while you're here. I'd do it straight away.'

'My darling,' I said, laughing, 'I couldn't afford a check-up in Australia. I don't have the insurance. I'm fine, really. Just a bit tired.'

'Hold on,' he said. Ten minutes later he came back and wrote a name and address on a piece of paper which he gave me: Dr John McCusker, St Margaret's Hospital. 'A friend of mine,' he said. 'He's a top surgeon, and he's willing to see you at eight tomorrow morning. He's a lovely man. Go. It won't cost you anything. You've got nothing to lose.'

I didn't want to go to a hospital. Hospitals give me the heebie-jeebies. But there was something about the way he looked at me that disturbed me and made me agree.

Dr McCusker was indeed a lovely man, tall and casually dressed in summer sportswear. He had beautiful eyes which were full of warmth and humour. He examined me thoroughly. 'I can feel a mass here,' he said, gently pressing my pelvic area. Afterwards he talked to me very kindly. It was arranged that I should have a scan first thing next morning.

I went home with Dan and Lois, had a cup of tea and one of my favourite nut biscuits and tried to watch television. But the biscuit stuck in my throat and I couldn't concentrate. Eventually I went to bed.

The scan revealed that I had a large tumour embedded in my pelvic wall, and that it was beginning to wrap itself around the lower end of the bowel. 'You've been carrying this around for a long time,' Dr McCusker said. 'We can't waste any more time. I want to operate this morning.'

I looked at him for a long time. 'But I've got no money,' I said. 'I wouldn't be able to pay you.'

Dr McCusker took my hand. 'What day comes after March the second?' he asked.

'March t'urrd.'

'And what month of the year is March?'

'The t'urrd.'

'So what does that make it?'

'The t'urrd of the t'urrd.'

Dr McCusker turned to the radiologist who had done my scan. 'How could we ask for money from someone with a lovely accent like that!' he said with a grin.

That night my dreams were confused and terrifying. Faces leered down at me. 'She deserves it,' one of them kept saying. It was the doctor at the Adelaide Hospital in Dublin, the one who'd tended to me when I'd broken my arm and my leg running away from the orphanage. But I knew he wasn't a doctor . . . he was one of the four who'd raped me. And now he was going to take away my baby. 'She deserves it. She deserves it . . .'

I woke up as I had done so often in the past, sweating, memories screaming in my head and in my body. Pain. Violation. The birdlike feel of Mammy's body as I lay on top of her in St Kevin's Hospital, begging her not to die. The warm wetness

89

as the bright gobbets of blood pumped from her mouth on to my pink Confirmation frock.

I was sobbing like a child. For Thomas, my lost baby. And my other babies, Nicolas, Androula, Helenita. Would I ever see them again? I'd spoken to them so reassuringly on the telephone last night, but now I wanted to see their faces. I wanted to hold them and kiss them, and tell them how much I loved them. How grateful I was to them for their big hearts and how proud I was of them for what they'd made of their lives. I wanted to say sorry to them for all the bad things that had happened to them when I was with their father. But more than anything, I wanted to hold them.

I thought of the children in Vietnam. What would happen to them if anything happened to me? The Foundation wasn't ready to carry on without me. I had to keep on fund-raising. Surely, after all those years of pain and suffering, this couldn't just be the end?

As the dawn came slowly up I put my life in God's hands. I knew that Dr McCusker would do the very best he could, but in the end it was God who would be watching over me. I was sure of it, and I asked him to take care of me.

Late next evening, soon after I had regained consciousness, Dr McCusker came to see me. The operation had caught the tumour just in time. I knew he had saved my life.

Eight days later I left hospital to stay with another new friend, Gaby Hollows, in Randwick, another pleasant suburb of Sydney. Dr McCusker came to see me every day, but I was still in continuous excruciating pain. I had to crawl across the floor from my bed to the bathroom. Dan would hear my gasps and moans and come in to help me out of bed and back. Eventually he was so worried he put a mattress on the floor and slept in my room.

I could no longer move. Dan helped me to the toilet day

and night by putting his hands under my armpits and dragging me across the floor. I felt so ashamed. I couldn't even cry aloud. The right side of my body was agony. I'd had many operations but I had never felt such pain as this.

'You must tell the surgeon,' Dan said.

'But he's been so kind to me,' I said, 'and he did the operation for nothing. I don't feel I've got a right to complain.'

But by the fourteenth day I couldn't take it any longer. I told Dr McCusker, who sent me immediately to see Professor Bennet at St Vincent's, a huge Sydney teaching hospital. After injections of local anaesthetic had failed to numb the pain Professor Bennet decided to operate next morning.

I woke in the ward to find Dan sitting beside me. I tried to speak but I could only whisper: 'Thank you for being here, Dan. I'm sorry about all this on your first trip out of Vietnam.'

He smiled and said 'It's okay,' and I was grateful.

Professor Bennet explained that he had had to remove a gastric nerve. The pain was gone. I was alive again. I thanked God. Then I phoned the children, and I phoned Vietnam. The staff sent me a message. 'We love you, Mama Tina. Come home and we look after you. We don't want to lose you from Vietnam.'

Dr McCusker told me very firmly that I mustn't fly for eight weeks, but within three weeks I was on my Australian tour again. I'm not proud of it, but I had no alternative. I simply had to find money for the children and I had a growing staff to pay.

The warmth of the Australian people reached out to me. I appeared on television and radio, gave interviews to papers and spoke to audiences across Australia in churches and local halls. Everyone wanted to help. Back in Sydney I was introduced to two people who were to become a great support to me and to the Centre, Janete Davenport who I met through one of her friends at Channel 7, and a high-powered dentist called Sandra Short.

I discussed with Dr Short the desperate need for a children's dental clinic in Ho Chi Minh City. Neglect and a poor diet were responsible for horrifying tooth decay in most of the children we saw. Dr Short listened with great interest, but made no promises.

I also discussed with Janete and Dr Short the possibility of setting up an office in Australia and they agreed to help. The Centre and its growing network of offices were now officially known as 'The Christina Noble Children's Foundation'. It had a solid ring to it, and after my welcome in Australia I felt more optimistic about the future.

I flew back to Vietnam with two hundred stitches inside me. Physically I felt weak and exhausted. I was eating very little, but my weight seemed to be increasing at an alarming rate, and I couldn't understand why.

ELEVEN

Our bank account was beginning to look healthier after my Australian tour, and more donations were gradually trickling in. My makeshift office systems would no longer do, and we found an accountant, cheerful and unflappable Mr Hai. I knew that our accounts must be properly audited, but auditors were expensive.

I phoned Mr Trinh Dinh Ban, a lawyer whose sister-in-law, Madame Oanh, had been kind to me when I first arrived in Vietnam. Madame Oanh was in her seventies and she had been in love with an American who had died very suddenly in the United States after the war. Before leaving for the last time he had written the words of a song on a piece of paper that she still kept. Madame Oanh and I used to hold hands on the back of a Honda and sing it: 'For ever and ever, my heart will be truuuuue. Sweetheart, for ever, I'll wait for youuuuu.'

Within an hour of talking to Mr Trinh Dinh Ban I had a call from Don Lam, a Canadian of Vietnamese origin who was general manager at Coopers & Lybrand in Saigon. It was the start of a happy working partnership. Coopers looked at our books and agreed to do our auditing at a very reduced rate.

Later Ernst & Young offered us their services free and we accepted, because every penny counted, but I missed Don Lam, and I was always grateful to him for helping when no one else was prepared to.

Almost out of the blue a computer and a bright red fridge arrived from Vets with a Mission, in America. Now we had cold water to drink, and Mr Hai set about computerizing our accounting systems. Within a few months a shipment of dental equipment also arrived from Dr Short, soon followed by Dr Short herself and two volunteer Australian dental nurses. Within a few weeks they had examined over a hundred children. Dr Short said she had never seen such bad teeth: almost all the kids were in serious dental trouble. Before she left Dr Short helped us set up a permanent dental clinic which we began to run in the outpatients' clinic three days a week.

One day that summer Lap was brought back to the Centre. I hardly recognized him. He looked confused and unhappy, and he had lost a lot of weight. He settled back into his old routines, playing on the computer and pottering about in the office, looking through the piles of educational books we kept there. But there was something subdued about him. It seemed to me that he was walking strangely, and that his balance was bad. Lap couldn't tell us in words what he was feeling, but he didn't have to. I knew he was fearful that he would be sent away again, and no amount of love could reassure him. I prayed that one day he would find a family who would love him as I did, but the prospect of that seemed remote in Vietnam.

There were so many maimed and disabled children in Ho Chi Minh City. In one of the poorest districts, I discovered a home run by a blind man called Mr Thanh. It was a terrible place, a dark shack down an alleyway with bars across the doors, a real breeding-ground for TB and all kinds of other things.

None of the children in Mr Thanh's home could see and some of them had even been born without eyes. They lay on top of one another in this black hole, forty-five of them, day after day. A few had been taught by Mr Thanh to make baskets, and foreign tourists sometimes came to see them and to praise Mr Thanh's heroic efforts in keeping the home going. The tourists gave money. This was Mr Thanh's private charity.

I had spoken about these children to the German ambassador to Unesco, Madame Ohoven. A German film crew had even come to Vietnam to make a film about them, and as a result money had been raised to build the children a properly adapted home. Mr Thanh was very excited, but his excitement turned to annoyance when he learned that the money was not going to be handed directly to him.

'You know this is quite a large sum of money, Mr Thanh,' I said, 'and it will only be given if this project is done correctly.' But Mr Thanh refused to co-operate unless he was put in charge of building the home himself.

Dan and Helen and I went to see him again. I said, 'Mr Thanh, there is no way you can allow the children to continue living in these shocking conditions. This building is a breeding-ground for diseases. Don't you want the children to have a decent house? It seems very odd to me.' Mr Thanh was still unmoved.

Meantime the money was lodged with Unesco and from time to time I would get a message from their representative, Dieter Barestricher: 'The money from Germany is waiting. All we need now is a proposal from the Foundation.'

'Okay, if you don't want to move away from here,' I suggested to Mr Thanh, 'what if we rebuild the house you're living in now and make it better?' Mr Thanh still refused.

I wrote to the People's Committee for the District but it was hopeless, our hands were tied. Mr Thanh was a private individual who had taken on the care of these children, so nothing, it seemed, could be done. Every time I visited, the children's condition seemed to be worse.

Since returning from Australia I'd felt weak and irritable. My body seemed puffy and overweight, and I was always thirsty. One night I fell into bed about ten o'clock, but I just couldn't get warm – my hands and feet felt icy, though my head was on fire. I lay there, my heart palpitating, telling myself to relax, and sliding in and out of blackness which I knew was unconsciousness, not sleep.

I was frightened and slid out of bed, but my legs were shaking and I couldn't stand. I caught sight of myself in the mirror. Earlier in the day Helen had mentioned that my lips looked blue. My face in the mirror looked drugged, and my lips did seem to have a bluish tinge. By now it was one o'clock. I dragged myself to the phone and called my doctor, Philip Barrow, who advised me to go to hospital immediately. Then I managed to phone Dan, who called me a taxi.

I arrived clutching a large bottle of water, and every few minutes I'd take a swig. I was thirsty, so thirsty. The hospital doctor tried to take it away from me. My temperature was very high, but my blood pressure was abnormally low, and the doctor wanted to keep me in for observation. But I'd had enough of hospitals and I clung on to my bottle, insisting I'd soon be all right.

Tests over the next few days revealed a possible abnormality in my kidneys, but otherwise the doctors seemed baffled. Dr Barrow advised me to go back to England for a proper rest. In my mind's eye I saw a quiet English room, with a comfortable bed and big soft white pillows. There was a smell of cut grass drifting through the window and outside the birds were singing. I had no responsibilities. Someone else was making all the decisions, someone else was taking care of me.

When had I ever had anyone to take care of me? I was so tired in Vietnam, and often so lonely. Always the same heat, always the same problems. I knew the English room was a fantasy. As the weeks passed I gradually began to feel a little better.

Now I received a letter from a man with long experience of working for humanitarian causes, offering to become our administrator for a very low salary. Once again, I thought, God was stepping in. With someone like this to take over the day-to-day running of the Foundation I could spend more time with the children, get well, and think about new ways to raise money.

My brush with this man was a nasty experience, but a useful lesson. He had a wide grin and a plausible manner. But he had not been with us long before word got back to me that he liked little boys. I couldn't believe it – a man with a long record as a humanitarian worker! This simply couldn't be true. But when I checked out the stories, the evidence began to add up.

One day I saw him having a game of rough and tumble with two of the young boys from the Sunshine School. He had his shirt off and as they rolled around he grabbed one of the boys and held him tightly. I knew this wasn't ordinary play. There was something sexual going on. The children knew it too, because afterwards they talked to some of my Vietnamese colleagues about it. Stories were also coming in from the children on the streets.

I was shattered. The Foundation was a place where children believed they were safe, and this man was betraying their trust. He had obviously imagined that because I was a woman on my own, he could take advantage of the situation.

I felt ill and depressed and weak, but I knew I had to confront him. I went to the office. The man towered over me, and I asked him to sit down.

Suddenly all my fury burst to the surface. 'You're a pae-dophile,' I said. 'I want you out of this office and out of Vietnam in the next twenty-four hours. You disgust me. You thought you could safely come here and abuse children because I'm just a woman on my own. You've got it wrong for once. I'm going to make sure you never work with children again. Now get out!'

I was shaking, and he'd turned white. I thought he was going to vomit. But then he pulled himself together and gave me some story about people spreading rumours because he had once worked for the CIA.

'Bollocks!' I said. 'Get out.'

Next morning I was in the office when he came to collect some bits and pieces. 'I'm going,' he said. Then he looked straight at me with a nasty, threatening smile, moving his eye-brows up and down. 'Just remember,' he said, 'I have an assas-sin's mind. I plot against my enemies. It may take six months, two years, ten years to get them' – here he held up his hands, striking the numbers off on his fingers – 'but I always remem-ber, and I always win.'

A verbal message was passed to me a few months later to the effect that if I told anyone what had happened he would sue me. I sent a message back: 'Go ahead! Open your own can of worms!'

I never heard from this man again and I understand he has now been blacklisted by humanitarian organizations. But the incident showed me that I could never be too cautious.

Christmas was coming. There were little carts selling cards and tinsel outside the big Catholic Cathedral of Notre-Dame, and there was a feeling of excitement everywhere. People rode round on Hondas with fully decorated Christmas trees on the back. We decided we would have a big Christmas party. The staff and the children went over the top getting ready. We had a big Christmas tree with lights near the front entrance to the Centre, all kinds of people and organizations in Ho Chi Minh City donated toys, clothes, bicycles and other things for prizes, and Vietnamese entertainers volunteered to come free of charge.

The party itself was fantastic. Hundreds of children and poor families came, and there were games, food, singing, Vietnamese dances, and several Father Christmases. Everyone enjoyed themselves. But for me there was a shadow. I had become increasingly worried about Lap and he was to undergo hospital tests.

TWELVE

My AUTOBIOGRAPHY WAS now to be published in the UK and I flew to London where I was welcomed by my publisher, John Murray, and my editor Caroline Knox. As I got ready for yet another round of talks and interviews I dreaded it. I ached from head to foot and I was continually tired. But, for the children's sake, I was desperate to make the most of this chance.

I saw my GP in Woking who told me that I should rest for a year, somewhere as far away from the office as possible, preferably with no phone. 'Some hope!' I thought. She also told me I was malnourished. 'But I can't be,' I said, 'I'm fat!' 'You may be,' she said, 'but that doesn't mean your body is getting enough vitamins.' She referred me to a nutritionist who put me on a special diet, but I still ached agonizingly.

Things were moving in London. Enterprise Oil were still supporting us and, thanks to Graham Hearne the Chairman, and Ray Dafter the Director of Corporate Affairs, the company had given us space in their London office to set up a British headquarters, manned by volunteers. With the interest produced by the book and my visit, it was being flooded with requests for information. We decided we needed a full-time manager. In England we now also had an extremely professional board of directors, and with their help I placed an advertisement in a professional magazine for a retired person to take on the job. One of the applicants was Michael Hunt.

As soon as I met Michael I knew I liked him. He was a man of means but he had no interest in expensive yachts or cars. His passion, I discovered, were the two magnificent cinema organs he had installed at his home. He loved their rich sounds and the romance of their history. I also learned that, like many people who are drawn to help others, Michael had had a tragedy in his life. Right from the start he did fantastic work for the Foundation, and when I was feeling low he always had a way of making me feel better. When he moved on two years later he continued to support the Foundation and became a loyal friend.

A member of the London Board, Laura Lindsay, had the brilliant idea of finding corporate sponsors for lectures in aid of the Foundation at the Royal Geographical Society. They were an immediate success. All kinds of high-profile people agreed to lecture, including Sir Fitzroy Maclean and Jonathan Dimbleby. The lectures are still going today, and they make a big financial contribution to our work.

I was happy during this time in England. The Foundation was becoming established, I felt that people were beginning to hear my message, and if I had had any doubts about telling my story they had now completely disappeared. The book's English title was *Bridge Across My Sorrows* and for many of the people who wrote to me, and came up to me on my tours, it seemed to have been just that.

'I've never been able to talk about it,' a rape victim wrote to me. 'It's been like a cancer inside me, an abscess poisoning me.

But when I read your book, I cried for the first time, and stopped hating and blaming myself.'

'I had a child who was taken away from me for adoption,' wrote another woman. 'I am sixty-seven years old and I've lived with the secret, and the grief of my loss, all my life. Now I have shared my secret with my husband. I was so afraid, but I read your book and I thought, if you have the courage to talk about it, so have I.'

In Birmingham a girl of eighteen came up to me. She told me that as a child she had been brutally abused by her grand-father and had given birth to a baby. She had never been able to tell her parents the truth, and her grandfather had taken a sadistic delight in playing grandparent to the little boy while her parents looked proudly on. Twice she had tried to commit suicide. When her grandfather died, everyone else grieved. 'I just wanted to take a knife and stab him in his coffin and scream out the truth about him,' she said. 'I couldn't, I was too afraid. But now I've read your book. I've read it over and over.'

I put my arms around her and held her. For she and count-less others, reading my book seemed to have broken through their isolation.

When I saw my own children, as usual we talked non-stop, laughed and often had a cry. Helen was now very successful as a singer and songwriter who had travelled the world. Like me, Helen was born with music in her soul, and by the age of twenty-one she already had a recording contract. Now she'd been voted Best International Female Singer, and her song 'Summer of Love' was in the European charts.

Helen is like fire and Androula like water, calm and deep. I knew she had been strongly affected by the knowledge of what I had suffered. Already a published poet and with a first-class Literature degree, Androula had decided she wanted to help others. She was now a trained social worker, and her partner

Michael, who she had met at university, was training as a social worker too.

Nicolas had graduated from college with a degree in business and finance and he and Sara, his Australian girlfriend, who he had met while he was visiting Helen in America, were planning to marry. Nicolas had great sympathy and understanding. I knew he was pondering what to do with his life.

One day he seemed very thoughtful. After a while he said, 'Mom, I've decided I want to come and work with you in Vietnam.'

I felt a lump in my throat. 'Why?' I asked.

'Mom, you've done so much for me. I was the first child you saved. You helped me find my dignity again. I know you saved my life. You need help now and I want to do something for you.'

It was hard for me to speak. 'Well,' I said after a while, 'you may be my son, but you'll still have to be approved by the Board in London, just like anyone else.'

'I know, Mom,' he said. Since then Nicolas has always stood beside me.

One of Androula's poems is called 'My Mother's House'. It is one of my favourites:

> I have to walk through spiders' webs
> when I visit my mother's house;
> They cling to my face like a warm hand
> whose fingers have found their way into my mouth.
>
> I never know which room she is in,
> but I always know she is there.
> I listen out for her heartbeat

and find it in my fingertips,
beating, like a small hard-skinned drum,
whose face is wind-dried and slow-sunned.

If I blow up at the ceiling her words fall
down to me,
but dissolve on my tongue
before I have even tasted them,
or fly out the high dusty windows
free as children.

Once, I heard her laughing in the garden
and caught a glinting glimpse of her,
dragging her mud-caked soul across the grass,
from which old secrets flew up to the moon-shy sky
in startled whispers.

As my plane left the tarmac at Heathrow and lifted off into
the blue, I thought with love and gratitude about my children.
We might have preferred to undo the past, but it was the past
that had bound us so closely together.

THIRTEEN

THERE WAS BAD news about Lap. Tests had shown that he had a tumour which was pressing on his spine. A difficult and delicate operation was needed to remove it, and there were no facilities for that in Vietnam. Without it he was going to die.

We immediately contacted our offices abroad, and within a few weeks an Australian lawyer named Steven Klinger phoned. He had persuaded the Royal Alexandra Hospital for Children in Sydney to do the operation free of charge, and Qantas had agreed to fly Lap to Australia. In July we saw Lap and Chief Nurse Lam off at Tan Son Nhat Airport. He looked very small. I knew he would be getting the best treatment, and when the operation was over he was going to convalesce with Steven Klinger's family. Thank God for good people like that, I thought. But it was very hard to have to send Lap away again.

The operation saved Lap's life, but the tumour had damaged his spine. We were told that he would never be able to walk again. Lap was being asked to face one tragedy after another. He became deeply attached to people, and he had grown to love Australia and the Klinger family. Now he was returning in a wheelchair to an uncertain future in Vietnam.

So many children who came to the clinic needed surgery that we were often in despair. Everything had to be paid for, though we were often helped by surgeons like Dr Du Perrier at the Alain Carpentier Heart Institute in Ho Chi Minh City. The Heart Institute is a humanitarian hospital founded by a Frenchman, and it charges according to what patients can afford, but there is a great demand for its services. It was Dr Du Perrier who saved the life of our darling Rosie.

Rosie had a terrible history. She'd been found buried in a rubbish dump in Quang Minh, which is a very poor province in the north of Vietnam. A little boy who was helping shovel refuse ready for burning noticed a tiny hand sticking out from under one of the piles. When she was taken to the local centre for orphaned children she was obviously dying.

A Hanoi hospital then referred her to Dr Du Perrier, who saw that she urgently needed open-heart surgery. But she was no bigger than a kitten, and he knew that she would never survive the operation in that condition. So Rosie was brought to us to see if we could help her to gain weight. When she arrived she was hovering between life and death and her skin had a frightening blue tinge, but gradually her weight began to climb. After a few weeks it was just over eight kilos, and Dr Du Perrier was able to do the operation she needed to seal the hole in her septum.

During the next two weeks we visited Rosie every day in the hospital. She was a beautiful baby, with feathery black hair and intense black eyes. Gradually her cheeks changed from blue to pale to pink and Rosie began to smile. When she came back to the Centre she was everyone's darling. Seeing her every day was like watching a beautiful flower unfolding. She went on growing steadily, and miraculously she seemed to have suffered no complications. Within three months Dr Du Perrier had given her a clean bill of health.

Under Vietnamese law, all children must return to their province as soon as they are medically fit to do so. So Rosie was taken back to the children's centre in Quang Minh, where we hear she is developing normally. We always knew that she would have to return to Quang Minh, but I think for all of us a bit of our hearts went with her when she left.

It is often difficult to face the day when children have to leave us. Many of them have such fighting spirit that it is infectious. Little blind Le Le is one of those, and when the time came for her to return to Ca Mau we were all in tears. She had grown into an adorable, confident little girl who loved to sing and dance. Because of her condition her eyes bulged severely, and we knew that we could never give Le Le back her sight, though it might be possible for her to have cosmetic surgery later on.

Le Le's home province of Ca Mau is several days' drive from Saigon. We travelled with Le Le south into the heart of the Mekong Delta, where the paddy fields are like lush green lawns. The Vietnamese countryside is very tranquil and beautiful, full of coconut and banana and mango trees, but in the Mekong crops are often destroyed by flooding, and Ca Mau is very poor. We had to cross three rivers to get there, putting the van on an ancient ferry each time. We felt we were taking Le Le a very long way away from us.

At first we were shocked by the children's centre. It was a grim, dilapidated concrete block with barely a stick of furniture, and the staff told us that the allowance for each child was the equivalent of 3 cents a day – barely enough for the most basic food. But there was love for the children oozing out of the place. Most of the street children in Vietnam are in the south, but jobs in children's centres tend to go to people from the north. Because Ca Mau is so remote the staff there are local people, and we could see that they really cared about the children.

107

I offered to increase the children's daily allowance, and to help with repairing the buildings. I also promised the director I would register the children on our sponsorship programme, which links children to sponsors in the West. So this was not to be the end of Le Le's story, nor of our relationship with the children's centre in Ca Mau.

One day I had a phone call from one of the street children. He sounded upset and asked me if I could come quickly down to Pham Ngu Lao. He told me that his friend Dinh had overdosed on heroin and no hospital would take him in. A doctor and I hurried down to Pham Ngu Lao. Dinh was in a terrible state. His eyes were rolling in his head, he was gagging and his whole body was shaking. We managed to get him into an ambulance and persuaded a hospital to take him in, which they did for one night, pumping his stomach out and putting him out on to the street again first thing in the morning.

I already knew Dinh. His legs were paralysed and he travelled round on a kind of home-made wooden skateboard with wheels attached. He had the round, rather innocent face of a country boy, and he didn't seem streetwise like many of the other kids. I knew he had a drug problem, and the other children told me that he was often picked up by the police, bombed out of his brains. I also knew that he had a tragic history of involvement with the paedophile sex trade.

I found Dinh again and brought him back to the Centre. He told me he came from Hue, in central Vietnam, about 600 kilometres from Saigon, and that he'd been crippled by polio since he was a very young child. Two years earlier, when Dinh was fourteen, his mother had remarried and had moved away and left him, so Dinh had travelled on his board all the way from Hue to Saigon, begging for food along the way. It had taken him about three months.

He said that after Hue, Saigon had seemed exciting, but he

wasn't used to the big city and he'd quickly got hooked on drugs. Soon he had had to steal to supply his habit. But now he really wanted to give up drugs and have some kind of normal life again and go to school. What he really wanted was a family, he told me. As he said this he was crying. I knew from experience that many children in Dinh's situation become suicidal.

I asked Dinh if he would be willing to go on a drug rehabilitation programme. 'Do you think you could do it?' I asked. Dinh nodded emphatically. I could see that he meant it, and that he was very determined. But I was worried about what was going to happen afterwards. Unfortunately there is a widespread drug culture in Vietnam which comes down from the older generation. Many of them grew up smoking opium, and children are exposed to drugs on a daily basis. The streets of Saigon are no place for a sixteen-year-old who is trying to kick a drug habit. Dinh needed somewhere to live and some support.

We had been negotiating with the People's Committee for a house in District 10, which they agreed to let us have rent free. It was a good family house on two floors, with a roof terrace and an extra room at the top. Downstairs there was a big sitting-room and a kitchen, and upstairs two big rooms. It suited what I had in mind – a shelter for boys like Dinh, with staff around, where we could try to reunite the boys with their families if that was what they wanted, or give them a chance to settle down and start learning something. We spruced it up and painted it and made two dormitories on the upper floor. The room on the top floor I thought could be a room for studying and homework, and I put a ping-pong table in downstairs.

That year after our Christmas festivities, we had another celebration. The Shelter in District 10 was officially opened on 26 December, and during the next few months twenty children, including Dinh, moved in. I thought of it as a nest, where children could shelter and then stretch their wings and eventually learn how to fly.

Dinh stayed at the Shelter until he was seventeen. He went back to school and at the end of a year he felt steady enough to move out into lodgings of his own. We helped him find a job at a diamond factory with a very good reputation for employing disabled people, and he's still there and working hard. He has friends, and he hasn't gone back on to drugs. He's a free spirit, he always will be, and he still likes to take off and wheel around the country, though now he goes by bus. But he always comes back, because for him the Foundation is his family and his home.

FOURTEEN

In the New Year I had a phone call from Nicolas and Sara. They had been approved by the Board and now they were ready to come to Vietnam.

As they walked towards me at Tan Son Nhat Airport they looked such a beautiful couple – Nicolas, with his dark Latin looks, and Sara, so graceful with her long shiny brown hair. I was thrilled to see them – the first members of my family to come to Vietnam!

Since there wasn't room for them in my tiny apartment, I'd rented a small house for the three of us in District 10. I begrudged spending any money that could be going to the Foundation, so the house was a cheap one. Panicked at the thought that Nick and Sara would soon be arriving I'd looked at it in a hurry – just buzzed round, taking in the size of the rooms and saying 'Fine, fine, this'll do grand' to the landlord. The house was up a side lane, which led to the back of the local hospital, a stone building which had orginally been whitewashed but was now a rather dismal grey.

District 10 is a somewhat characterless area, with dimly lit streets and very few shops. As we drove to the house it was raining, and the pot-holes in the lane had turned into puddles. We tried to talk cheerfully, but gloom set in when we realized why the house had been so cheap. Its front overlooked the hospital mortuary.

That night the rains were lashing, the wind was howling and there were rolls of thunder. When I woke in the night to go to the toilet I saw from the window that there was a black van outside the mortuary. The door of the mortuary was open and figures were moving about. Lit by flashes of lightning, it looked like a scene from *The Body Snatchers*. I ran to the light switch and as I set off downstairs rats and cockroaches scuttled in all directions.

Next morning Nicolas said, 'Mom, I hope you haven't signed any papers yet for this place.'

'Yes, I have.'

'For how long?'

'Six months.'

Nicolas swallowed. 'Do you know where our water's coming from?'

'No.'

He pointed to a big black tube which ran along the ground from a hole outside. 'There. And do you remember what you saw running into that hole last night?'

'A rat,' I said. 'God above! I'm going to see if we can get our money back and move out of here quick!' But the landlord wouldn't give us our money back, so we had to stay where we were for six months. Nicolas and Sara had smartly chosen the back bedroom but mine faced straight into the mortuary yard. I bought the thickest material I could find to make curtains, and kept them closed.

Sara and I shivered every time we saw a black van drive into the yard of the mortuary, either to deliver or take away, and in the tropical heat the smell was often terrible – I'm sure they

. 'Mama Tina's back!' The children rushing for a hug, Helen in the background

2. An abandoned child found sleeping on a bridge in Ho Chi Minh City

3. On camera: Phuc's mother and I are filmed returning to the box which was once the family's home

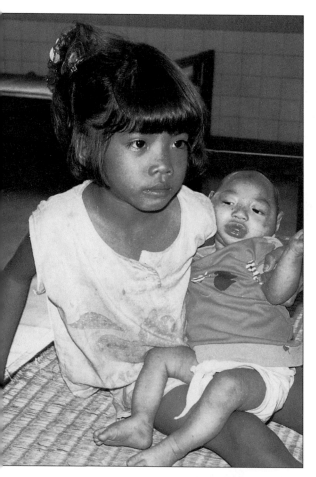

4. This little girl was caring for her malformed brother alone on the streets before they were brought to the Centre

5. In the market area: Helen Thuong and I speak to begging women whose babies are obviously drugged

6. Essential equipment arrive for the Centre from sponsors abroad

7. Nurses and children in the Special Care Unit

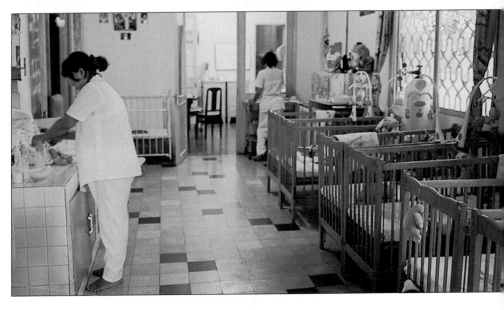

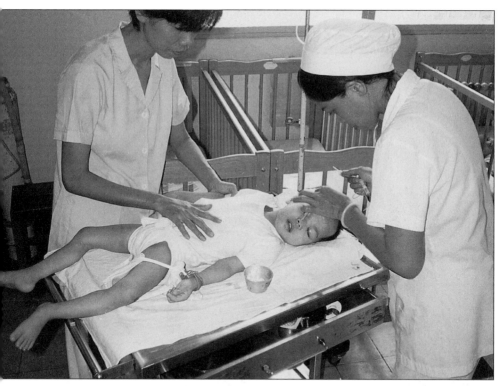

. An injection for a sick child in the Special Care Unit

. The nursery children do their morning *tai chi* exercises in the compound

10. Walking in a Saigon park with Nicolas and Sara

11. With Androula at the 1997 People of the Year Awards

12. Helen and her son Thomas

13. One of the classes at the Sunshine School

14. A bike is *every* Vietnamese child's dream. The proud owner of a bike donated to the Sunshine School

15. The Sunshine Football Team in the stadium

16. The Sunshine Choir

7. Oh we do love to be beside the seaside: on the beach at Vung Tau

18. Everyone gets a present at Christmas and a little box with Vietnamese cake

19. Ha and Nghia receiving their awards at the White Christmas Ball

20. Trung, soon after he began to walk

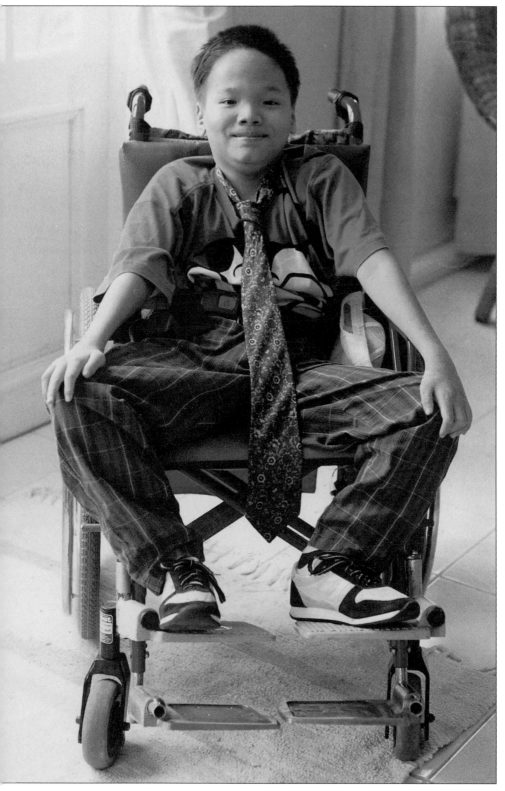

1. Lap at home in Scotland

22. The *ger* village under construction

23. Some of the prison
boys in Ulaanbaatar

24. Helga and friends
from the *ger* village on
their way to school

25. Wendy Evans with one of the children from the *ger* village

26. With the Irish President, Mary McAleese, at the launch of the Foundation in Ireland

27. Me, Kathy, Sean and Andy in the Marrowbone Lane flat, 1950

28. Sean and I with the Irish singer Mary Black

29. At my mother's grave in Mount Jerome Cemetery

had no refrigeration. It was a tough introduction to life in Saigon, but Nick and Sara got straight down to work, saying they hadn't come to Vietnam for a holiday. During their first week they stayed at the Centre till long after midnight painting the office. They gave it a real facelift, a whole new lease of life.

Nicolas took on the job of office manager, which he approached with his usual care and thoughtfulness. He sat down with the Vietnamese staff to hear their ideas and discuss how the running of the Centre could be improved. What was more he really listened. Sara helped us with the accounts and after a while she took over on the busiest day of the month, when families arrived to collect their sponsorship money. It was always a long day. We insisted that the child come with the family and we always talked to the children to hear how they were getting on.

But there was no getting away from the fact that socially Nicolas and Sara were finding Saigon boring. They enjoyed going to the cinema and the theatre, but there were no English plays or films, and the TV channels were all in Vietnamese. At that time there weren't even any subtitled British or American films.

'Why do you have this colour television, Mom?' Nicolas asked me one night. 'You know you don't really understand Vietnamese.'

'It's just for the colour and the noise,' I told him. 'Usually I'm living on my own, you know, and it helps me forget how lonely I am sometimes. I don't like to hear too much silence.' So Nicolas and Sara decided to buy me a video recorder – only to discover that there were no English-language videos to buy or rent in Saigon. 'That's the way it is,' I told them. 'That's Vietnam.'

One night Nicolas came home triumphantly waving a

video he'd found on the back shelf of a video shop. 'English language,' he announced, 'American – Julia Roberts – *Sleeping with the Enemy*.' Sara was as excited as I was. In fact we were like children at our first picture show.

We made our plans. On Saturday evening we'd all get home by six o'clock, have a lovely meal of spaghetti and baked potatoes with cheese, get a few boxes of popcorn, and watch the movie. In the heat and humidity of Saigon we were all exhausted, and work at the Centre was draining. The idea of a relaxing evening at home with an American video was heaven.

Everything went as planned. We ate our supper, then pulled up our chairs and poured out the 7-Up. 'We've got to do this right,' Nicolas insisted, handing out the popcorn and turning out the lights. The picture was a bit cloudy with a few lines running through it, but we didn't care.

Soon we were all engrossed. Julia Roberts was trying to escape from her violent husband – a familiar scenario for Nicolas and me. I was too absorbed in poor Julia's trauma to eat my popcorn and I was rooting for her all the way as she fled from one American town to the next with her husband in murderous pursuit. Would she escape the bastard?

Suddenly the screen went blank. We sat for a few seconds, waiting, but nothing happened. Nicolas checked the tape. 'Oh my God,' he said, 'it's only a one-hour tape. They've left the ending off.' Nicolas and Sara looked at one another and burst out laughing. But I didn't think it was funny. I was disappointed and furious. And I never did discover what happened to Julia.

A few months later we found another video shop that was renting out English-language films. They were *cheap*, too – only 4,000 dongs each, about 25 cents. Again we were terribly excited. We decided we'd rent *four* – they'd be a bit of security, something to watch when we really needed to forget about work. '*Great!*' we kept saying to one another. 'Isn't that really *great*?'

We weren't going to be taken for a ride this time, so we checked with the man in the video shop who even showed us the credits rolling at the end. 'You see ending? Film has ending, no problem,' he grinned.

We decided we'd make an evening of it, and invite some friends. The response from everyone was the same: 'An English film! Brilliant!'

Again we drew the blinds and handed round the popcorn. But as soon as the film started we realized something was wrong. The picture and the sound were okay, but the tape started halfway through the story. This time I was so mad I jumped up and leapt on to my bike. I pedalled like a mad-woman round to the video shop and ran inside. 'Listen, you,' I gasped furiously, 'this tape's only got half a film on it.'

The man smiled and nodded. 'Yes – only half.'

'Don't you smile at me,' I said. 'Where's the other half?'

'If you want other half you must pay.'

'Okay,' I said, 'let's have it. I've got a houseful of people sitting there waiting to see the beginning.'

He lifted the tape, looked at the title and shrugged. 'No, I not have. Foreigner rent first half and take up to house in An Phu.'

'Did the foreigner *know* he was only renting the first half?' I almost screamed at him. 'I'll bet he didn't, sweetheart! I'll bet he'll soon be down to give you a clip around the ear. Don't you *know* what these videos mean to us?'

He shrugged again. 'When foreigner bring back, I give you. But sometime foreigner forget and not bring back.'

'Look,' I said, 'a film is a film, right? Even if it's on two videos, it's still one film.'

'*Two* film,' he insisted.

'No, it's just that you've got it in two halves, but it's still one film. *One* story.'

'No. Foreigner have Part One. You have Part Two.'

I cycled home. We decided to try another video.

The Piano – no ending.

The Scarlet Letter – no beginning.

My Left Foot – no sound.

After that when we rented a video we always made sure to ask: 'You have Part One and Part Two? Does it have sound?'

Often the answer was, 'Sorry, no, we have Part Two, but no Part One.'

It's much easier to get English-language videos in Vietnam now, but it's still very hard to get them with an ending.

FIFTEEN

In THE OFFICE one morning I was going through some paper-work when I heard a commotion of voices, some of them sounding distressed. Downstairs I found a group of clinic staff. They all looked shocked and upset.

One of them was holding a bundle, wrapped in a cotton shawl. A tiny dark head was poking out, but when I drew close it looked more like half a head – there was an exposed and bleeding cavity where part of the scalp should have been. I saw a flash of white bone. I turned away. Surely this baby could not be alive. It would be better if it weren't.

The baby was alive, however. A tiny flame of life still flickered in her. Her body was a small skeleton hung with sagging skin that was red and raw and covered in scabies. 'Good God,' I thought, 'is it possible that a human being has done this to a child?' I felt ashamed to be human. I forced myself to look into the baby's face. Her eyes were half open, but they were dead. I knew she had given up, she was in agony and she wanted to die. Nicholas wept when he saw her.

Bé had been abandoned on a collective farm in the jungle area in Tan Hiep, not far from Saigon. She was found naked in a plastic bag and had obviously been there for some days. She had been literally eaten alive. Red ants and maggots had burrowed their way into her scalp and had begun to attack the rest of her body, and her injuries were terrible. She had septicaemia, she was gasping for breath, and our doctors found that her liver and her lungs were barely functioning.

There cannot have been a moment of baby Bé's life that had not been hell. She had been born from her mother's belly straight on to the street and a pimp had rented her out to another woman for begging, an all too common practice with unwanted babies in Vietnam. Bé was carted around in the blazing sun and the humid heat from early in the morning till late into the night. She was given Valium to keep her quiet, so that she was in a semi-coma. Finally, when she was dying from dehydration, she'd been put in a plastic bag and left in the jungle.

That day was the beginning of a long, long fight to save Bé – not just her poor, abused little body but her damaged soul. I believe Nicolas and Sara were the ones whose love finally gave Bé the will to survive. Nicolas couldn't forget his first sight of her. He was deeply affected, and kept thinking and talking about her. Over the next few weeks he and Sara took time every day to go and sit with Bé in the Special Care Unit. I'd see their two heads bent together over her cot as they sat looking down at the frail little body, which was full of tubes and wires.

Eventually Bé progressed enough to be taken off the drip, and her terrible wound began to heal. Her skin gradually started to lose its angry, irritable redness, and with frequent, patient feeding she put on some weight. Day after day and week after week Nicolas and Sara went to see her. Now they could hold her and they would gently stroke her and talk to her. But when Bé opened her eyes they still seemed empty and far away. It was as if she had not yet crossed over into the land of the living.

Then one day when Nicolas picked her up, her body suddenly seemed to register the contact. She clung to him like a tiny monkey. That day we knew that Bé had made it. She had decided it was worth living, but it took many months before she started to show any real interest in human contact. When she did the bond between Nicolas and Bé grew closer and she would hold up her arms to him as soon as he came into the room.

May in Ho Chi Minh City was humid and blisteringly hot, and the house behind the mortuary was unbearable. The body has a hard time pumping blood round in such temperatures, and you feel as if your organs are cooking. The old air-conditioner in the Special Care Unit at the Centre was on its last legs, and I worried about the cost of replacing it. When I wasn't worrying about that I was worrying about the leaks in the roof, which needed repairing before the monsoon came. 'One step at a time, Christina. One step at a time,' I kept telling myself. Isn't that what He'd said? We'd come a long way since then. But sometimes I asked God if I would ever be free of this endless crippling worry. Would we always have to stagger on, hand to mouth? We had no regular income. Only the constant effort of fund-raising kept us going.

We decided to take the Sunshine children for a day out at the seaside at Vung Tau, which in French colonial times was the Riviera-style beach resort of Saigon. Vung Tau is down-at-heel these days, with a beach-front full of wooden shacks and stalls selling souvenirs and turtle shells, but it was heaven for the children. Most of them had never seen the ocean before. We went to the Marina, which is a clean beach, and they took to the sea like ducks to water. But as everyone splashed and paddled I kept thinking of the blind children in

Mr Thanh's shelter. We'd got no further with Mr Thanh and I felt depressed.

Eventually I managed to persuade Mr Thanh to let me take the children on an outing to Vung Tau. I shall never forget the expressions on their faces as they felt the sand between their toes and then the water lapping round their feet. They lifted their faces and sniffed the salty smell of the ocean and listened to the sound of the waves roaring and crashing. They were entranced. How could I return them to hell, I thought, but I knew I had to.

One weekend I had a strange encounter in Vung Tau. I was wandering along, dreaming about building a holiday house so the children could stay a few days instead of just a few hours, when I tripped. At my feet I saw a teenage boy lying on the sand. His legs were badly deformed, and he crawled aside on his belly, dragging his legs behind him. He held out his hand: 'You give me money.'

My heart went out to him, but I didn't show it because I knew it wasn't going to help.

'I never give money to beggars,' I said.

He half-turned his body, and suddenly his face broke into a wide grin of recognition. 'Ah, Mama Tina! I look you everywhere! Everybody I speak say "You know Mama Tina? When she come to Vung Tau?" Ah, I so happy! I no want money. I just want see Mama Tina.'

I smiled. 'Your English is very good.'

'Yes, I learn English so I can beg.'

'Do you want to beg all your life?' I asked.

'No, but I must. My legs no good.'

'Do you have a dream?' I said.

'My dream I one day walk again. Then I work in post office.'

'That's a great dream,' I said. I gave him my card and ten dollars. 'Can you come to see me on Monday, ten o'clock? I'd really like to help you, but I can't promise. All I can promise is that I'll try very hard. Okay?'

He took the ten dollars and nodded. 'Okay?'

I grabbed his hand in an Italian handshake and said 'OKAY!'

We both laughed and he crawled off.

Trung, as he was called, turned up at eight o'clock on Monday, two hours earlier than arranged. He told us he'd been born in central Vietnam, at a place called Nha Trang, which is famous for its beautiful beaches. He'd caught polio when he was three, and his parents had abandoned him a year later. He could only just remember them.

A single woman had taken Trung in then, cared for him and sent him to school, but she had died when he was ten. At this point Trung started to weep. 'She good lady,' he said several times. 'I still love her.'

From then on Trung was on his own. He couldn't stay at school, and there was no way he could earn money to buy food. His starved little body became weaker and weaker, and it was then that he started begging, crawling on his belly like a snake. He kept hoping that another kind lady would take him in, he said.

He heard there was an American doctor in Vung Tau who could help his legs and he travelled there from Nha Trang, but he soon discovered that this was just another story. In Vung Tau he survived by begging. He kept on studying English from a little book that the kind lady who'd died had given him. He said it helped to sharpen his mind. He showed us the book, which he still kept in his pocket.

But eventually Trung had become too tired to study and depression set in. Sometimes he cut his own arms with a piece of metal, he said, and he hoped that one day he would have the courage to cut his veins. He could see no future for himself.

'I no want to live like begging snake all my life,' Trung said, after he had told us his painful story. 'Mama Tina, please, you help me?'

We were all so pleased when the orthopaedic surgeon at the Rehabilitation Centre in Ho Chi Minh City agreed to examine Trung. The surgeon phoned to say that he believed that he could do a series of corrective operations to straighten Trung's joints and legs and within a few weeks Trung was admitted to hospital. My heart turned over when he said goodbye to us. I knew he was in for a lot more pain and difficulty. Trung knew that too, but he was such a brave boy, and now he was full of hope.

SIXTEEN

MORE AND MORE foreign journalists were asking to interview me or to come and film at the Foundation. I knew it all helped our fund-raising. And maybe, just maybe, I always thought, another documentary would help us to buy some computers. But these visits took up a lot of time. And there was so much administration to do.

The Foundation's work had increased enormously. As early as 1992 we had begun getting proposals from various Vietnamese organizations. It might be the Committee of Care and Protection for Children, or the Women's Union, or the Department of Labour for a particular province. The project they wanted our help with could be a school or a health clinic or a sports project or the digging of a well for a village. We also proposed projects where we saw they were needed.

Then the bureaucracy would begin. The proposal would have to be approved by the local People's Committee, then by the Ward Committee in the city, then it would probably have to go through a further committee, through MOLISA in Hanoi, and sometimes through the Ho Chi Minh department of MOLISA as well. Sometimes PACCOM, which is responsible for non–governmental organizations, would also be involved. There were numerous rules and regulations, and the process of setting up a project could take months or even years. I felt permanently tied up in loops of red tape. If I was working in Africa or South America I'd have none of this, I sometimes thought.

Dan and Nicolas and Sara did everything they could to ease the strain on me, and the Vietnamese staff in the office were a great team. They always stood staunchly by me and without their loyalty I couldn't have carried on. Sometimes, I knew, they stayed working late into the night. On difficult days, when my self-esteem hit rock-bottom and they could see that I was feeling low, they'd just come up to me and say very quietly, 'We love you, Mama Tina. You very good for our children.'

One person who could always make me feel better was Quoc. Quoc had been a driver at the Floating Hotel until Nicolas discovered that Quoc's ambition was to work with children. Officially he was now our minibus driver, but I think Quoc spent more time with the babies than he did behind the wheel. 'Can I help them read?' he was always asking. 'Can I show them how to draw?' He played football with the boys in the Shelter and helped them with their school work. If I couldn't find Quoc, I always knew where he was – he'd be playing with the children. Many of the children who came to us simply didn't know how to play. They'd never seen toys before.

This was where our volunteers could be so useful. There was certainly no shortage of applicants, but I'd learned to be very cautious. I'd realized that some of them had a hidden agenda – they were what the Americans call 'on the make'. One German who came for a few weeks seemed unusually clued up, and he was always at my side. 'He never misses a trick,' I observed to Dan. After a while I sussed out why. He had a tiny cassette-recorder in his top pocket and he was recording every word I said.

One day I turned abruptly and prodded him in the chest. 'I see you've got that little what-d'you-call-it going again. I can see the red light through your shirt.'

He went very red and had nothing to say. Later I discovered he'd kept recordings of everything, labelled and dated. He was secretly planning to write his own book. Fame, I was beginning to realize, had its drawbacks.

Two exceptional volunteers came to us that year – Lucia Ennis, a stunning Irish blonde, and Christine Byrne, an Australian teacher whose partner, Neill, had been posted to Saigon. After reading my book Lucia and her friends had raised over $4,000 with a sponsored hike in the pitch dark through the glens of County Wicklow. When she arrived and handed over the money I was touched.

I could see straightaway what a warm, generous person Lucia was. She was also determined, which you need to be as a volunteer. When I asked her if she'd like to stay she was torn. She went home to Ireland to think about it, but somehow I knew she'd be back, and I was right.

When Nick told me one morning that a woman called Christine Byrne had phoned it seemed like an omen. Christine Byrne – my maiden name! Before Neill's posting Christine had been working as a special education teacher in a Brisbane primary school, and now she found herself, by chance, living in a rented house right behind the Foundation. She'd read about us in the *Lonely Planet* guide, I discovered. Now there was fame!

Christine's experience was just what we needed. But I really saw the kind of person she was when one evening she dashed across the city to be with a little boy who was dying. He was such a sad little boy, an Amerasian who had been abandoned at birth and then unsuccessfully adopted. Christine was determined that he would not be left to die alone.

When she reached the hospital the staff were not sympathetic, but she spent the night with him, giving him oxygen to ease the pressure on his lungs, talking to him, caring for him. She wanted him to die with dignity, and she was there with him when he died. That was typical of Christine. To me that act alone made me grateful she had come to Vietnam.

Most days I seemed to be running here, there and everywhere. A Dutch television company arrived to make a film, and no sooner had I finished with them than a young London journalist, Robert Crampton of *The Times*, flew to Saigon to interview me and spend a week at the Foundation. When Robert arrived I was with a sixteen-year-old girl and her baby who had been brought in to the office. The girl had hidden her pregnancy from her family – she'd barely eaten for months and had wound a rope tightly round her stomach to keep it flat. The baby was distressed and malnourished, and they both urgently needed help.

There were many other emergencies that week, and Robert was obviously very affected by what he saw. On his last evening he said to me, 'Christina, this week's been an amazing experience for me, but you must be exhausted. Why don't you try and go home early tonight. Will you do that? Will you take some time off and go home now?'

I agreed, wearily. 'Okay.'

But I had other plans. As soon as I got home I rushed around, showered, dried my hair and slipped into white silk trousers and a shimmering gold shirt. I kept glancing at my watch. I knew Robert would be dropping in for a last drink at the Headliner Club, and sure enough, a couple of hours later he wandered in. His face was a picture when he saw me up on stage, neon lipstick ablaze . . .

You can shake an apple off an apple tree,
Shake it, baby, shake it, but you can't shake me . . .

As I belted out the song I kept glimpsing Robert and was
amused by his expression of total disbelief. All week he'd been
watching Mama Tina, now he was watching Mae West,
Tammy Wynette . . . when I was singing I could escape and
be anyone I wanted to be.

After I'd finished, Robert Crampton stood up, took his
handkerchief from his pocket and went round the tables,
saying, 'Please, put your hands in your pockets and give money
to this woman. She deserves it!' I liked Robert Crampton.

That year we received a visit from Mother Teresa. She and
her nuns had requested that they should have the use of a room
above my office where a priest would say Mass for them every
morning. At first the authorities refused to allow this, but
Mother Teresa seemed unruffled – she was quite prepared to
take her nuns outside to pray in the street – and the authorities quickly relented.

As we sat together one evening we spoke about Ireland.
Mother Teresa told me that although she had been born in
Yugoslavia she had done her training at the Loretto Convent
in Rathfarnham. She had happy memories of Ireland, she told
me, but she looked at me, deeply and sadly, when I told her
about my experiences at St Joseph's. She reached out and took
my hand and held it tightly in both of hers, and her eyes
seemed to be looking right into my soul.

We talked of Vietnam, and I told her how overwhelmed I
had felt at first by what I saw. I'd been ready for hardship, but
I had not been equipped for the extent of the pain and
suffering.

'And now?' Mother Teresa asked. 'How do you feel now?

'I've been deeply affected by the Vietnamese people,' I said.

'I've been humbled by their forgiveness and encouraged by their hope. I feel I've learned and developed since I came to Vietnam.'

Mother Teresa continued to hold my hand. It gave me a great feeling of peace. It was as if my mother was holding my hand again, and I didn't want her to let go. She left Tu Xuong Street as she had arrived, without any fuss. 'I will remember you and I will pray for you,' she said.

Sometimes, I was aware, people compared me to Mother Teresa, but I knew I was quite unlike her. She would be a saint one day, I thought, but I wasn't saint material. Our biggest difference, though, was that Mother Teresa believed Catholicism held the answer to everything. I didn't believe in 'isms'. I just knew we'd got to build a new world. And we'd got to start with the children.

SEVENTEEN

No rest for the wicked! I thought, as I read the itinerary. *Bridge Across My Sorrows* was now being published in paperback, and I had to set off across the world again. I knew I'd got to do my best to look smart when I stood up in front of those posh audiences, but mostly my wardrobe consisted of baggy white cotton trousers and white cotton tops. I wore them every day, they were so cheap and comfortable.

I sighed and had a little daydream about shopping in London, walking down Knightsbridge to Harvey Nichols and buying myself something *really* nice. Then I'd have coffee at Harrods, and then . . . 'Mom,' I could hear Nicolas calling. I focused again and went on with my packing. What the heck, I thought, they'd have to take me as I was.

I wasn't looking forward to this tour. After Mother Teresa's visit I'd felt calmer, as if I'd been able to close a troubled chapter of my life. The past was the past, and somehow I had survived it. I was Mama Tina now. I'd cried enough for little Christina Byrne from Dublin. But I knew I was going to have to weep for her all over again.

There were other things that hurt, too. I'd begun to realize that some people thought I jetted about just for the pleasure of it. How could I explain that I didn't like strange beds and anonymous airport lounges. What I really wanted was to be in hot, dirty Saigon working with the children. I wanted to hold them and comfort them, have fun with them, see them growing and achieving, I wanted to have time to think about new projects. But everything had to be paid for and that all depended on me. We couldn't afford to send out glossy brochures or employ marketing people, and in any case I didn't want to spend our money that way.

I also realized that as a child I'd had such bad experiences with adults that I'd separated the people who'd hurt me off in my mind, and I expected everyone else in the world to be like Doris Day. Now I was learning. These people who criticized me should see me now, I thought bitterly. And they should have seen me on that flight from Hong Kong!

I hate flying at the best of times, but I'd had Janete Davenport with me, on her way to spend some time at the Foundation as a volunteer. I always find travelling with Janete reassuring because she was once a flight attendant herself with an Australian airline.

As we approached Saigon that night everything seemed nice and peaceful. Then, just as we were about 200 metres short of landing at Tan Son Nhat, a freak storm hit the airport. The control tower went out of action and everything outside went black as the ace of spades.

'Jesus, Mary and Joseph!'

The pilot was struggling to take the plane back up. Inside the noise was horrendous. For what seemed like hours we were juddering from side to side and bucking up and down. It was like a roller-coaster.

There was no announcement – the captain had other things to worry about. The stewardesses sat strapped into their seats, their faces pale and stiff. All I could see around me were staring, terrified eyes, open mouths, ashen faces. A woman near me was clutching her husband and crying.

It got worse. The plane seemed to be falling and the noise was like racing cars taking the bends in a Grand Prix rally. I glanced at Janete. It must be all right, I thought. She knew about flying and she'd have said something if things were really dangerous.

Then I thought about my teeth. I've got a good set of pearls, always have had, but Mario had knocked out my back teeth in one of his rages and I'd had to have four false ones. I'd never liked them, but they were great for chewing. I didn't want them to get broken because I knew I couldn't afford another set.

I eased them out and held them in my hand. The roaring continued. Still no word from the captain. The storm was absolutely terrifying. 'Janete,' I said, 'is this normal what's going on? Have you ever experienced anything like this before?' Janete was sitting very upright, staring straight ahead. 'No' was all she said.

I wondered where would be the safest place to put my teeth. I thought perhaps Janete could advise me. 'Where do you think I should put my teeth?' I said. 'Shall I put them in my bag, or shall I put them in this pocket in front, or would it be better to put them back in my mouth?'

Janete didn't reply and I looked at her. She was as white as a ghost. My God! If Janete was frightened it must be serious! But I couldn't get the idea of my teeth out of my head.

'Did you hear me, Janete?' I said. 'You look awful pale. What'll I do with my teeth? I don't want them to get broken if the plane crashes or anything. It took me a long time to get them to settle in my mouth and fit properly without hurting.' I held them out to her. 'What'll I do with them, Janete?'

Janete turned on me. 'Do what you f——g like with them!' she hissed. 'I don't care what you do! Don't you f——g under-stand? If we go down it won't be your f——g teeth you need to worry about! Just say your prayers, for God's sake!'

What seemed like hours after that the pilot announced that he was going to try and land at Bangkok to refuel. Seven hours later than scheduled we finally made it to Tan Son Nhat Airport. Everyone in the plane was in shock. No one was capable of uttering a word.

We sat for a while. Janete slowly reached out and took my hand. Her beautiful red hair was limp and her eyes looked double their normal size. 'I'm sorry about your teeth,' she said. 'But I think I should tell you, Chris, that if it wasn't for the captain we wouldn't be here now. We've been so lucky.'

We tottered through the airport to find Helen and Quoc waiting for us by the checkout. They looked pale and anxious.

'They tell us your plane is lost. Where in the air you go?' Helen stuttered.

Quoc was visibly relieved. He grabbed our bags. 'Hello, hello, Mama. We worry. We think something terrible happen.'

'Something terrible *did* happen,' I said.

'I'm never going on an aeroplane again,' I told Janete as we all sat safely at home having a cup of tea.

But of course I had to. And now I was going off again. Yes, I wished those people could have been on that plane. That would have shown them how enjoyable jetting around can be.

Nick, Sara and Quoc took me to Tan Son Nhat. They stood, waving, as I walked slowly through into the departure area. I kept turning back to look at them until at last Quoc's kind dolphin face disappeared into the crowd.

Fortunately this flight was uneventful and, as always, Australia welcomed me. There were interviews, talks, chat shows, meetings with the helpers in the Foundation Office, an auction organized by the Overseas Dental Association that raised $22,000 – the adrenalin began to flow a bit.

New Zealand. South Africa. Yes, if it was Tuesday, I must be in South Africa. This constant need to travel and fund-raise made me feel as if water was being poured on my spirit. I wanted to spend time with the children in Vietnam, doing the things I knew I could do best. But I just couldn't be every-where at the same time.

A fax arrived from Nicolas.

Mom – It's looking good here. You won't recognize the office. We've reorganized everything – filing systems, accounts department. I sent out a wish-list to local businesses and we got a great response – five almost new grey desks, filing cabinets, a couple of cupboards, two more computers, a new printer. Enterprise Oil have given us lots of paper and files. Oh and guess what! A new fax machine arrived yesterday from the Bishop of Sydney. Do you remember he told you he'd dreamt about you years before you met?

Still lots more to be done but don't worry. Everything is being taken care of. The boys' shelter is doing fantastically well. The ping-pong table is Number One!

Important. We've had a letter from Holland, the Schumacher Foundation, someone called Henrietta Schaffer. Sounds a really nice woman, genuinely interested. They want to visit. I'll fill you in more when you come back.

We miss you. Please take it easy, and for God's sake stop worrying!

Love Nico and Sara

I read it over and over. I sensed things were changing for Nico and I felt happy. It was wonderful to hear him so involved.

After a week in South Africa I flew back to Sydney. At Rotary International's annual conference I described our new project to help starving families in Kaen Giang. Nico and one of the staff had been down to the Cambodian border and had been shocked by what they saw – families living in rural squalor with no fresh water, open sewers, skeletal children with gastro-intestinal disorders. These people had been abandoned and we were trying to set up a revolving loan programme to help them get back on their feet and become self-sufficient. I described how a tiny loan could enable a starving family to buy livestock, rice and seeds to farm the parcel of land the government had given them. The interest on the loan would be 2 per cent, to cover the running costs of the programme, and if the loan was repaid early there would be no interest at all. The family would then be self-supporting and the capital could be used to help a family in another poor village.

When I spoke I forgot my exhaustion, but when I got back to Janete's house I was so tired I fell asleep with my clothes on.

Next morning at 6.30 Janete put her head round the door, all bright and cheerful. 'Christina, I have a cup of tea for you in the kitchen.'

'Oh God,' I said. 'I don't want to get up. I just want to sleep and sleep and sle-e-e-p.'

'Oh, now come on, Christina. You've got that talk to give this morning. It's an important one, isn't it?'

I ducked my head under the bedclothes, like a child who didn't want to go to school. 'Tell me what clothes you need today and I'll get them out for you,' Janete persisted. 'I know you're tired, darling, but once you're under the shower you'll be all right.'

I loved Janete. She was so kind and tolerant. But just then I wished Janete and the world would go away.

134

EIGHTEEN

'THERE'S A CALL for you,' said the Australian talk-show producer, 'a lady who says she knows you.'

I picked up the receiver. 'Hello?'

'Hello, Christina.' It was a voice with an Irish accent. 'I was at St Joseph's in Connemara with you. It's Margaret. I bet you don't remember me.'

Margaret Merryman. Tallish, a little bit older than me, mid-length hair pulled back from her forehead, held by a clip at the side. Long legs that made her black shoes look less clumpy than mine.

'Yes I do,' I said. 'You're Margaret Merryman. How are you, Margaret?'

'I'm fine, just fine, very happy. I'm married to an Australian and I have a son. I thought your book was brilliant, Christina, but you were too soft on those nuns. Remember how they shaved your head? Sure, they gave you an awful life.'

'I know,' I said, 'I know.'

'And didn't they beat the hell out of us! I'll never forgive them. If I ever write about them I won't be as soft as you were, believe me. I'm a *Baptist* now, you know, and I take no nonsense from anyone. I stand up for myself.'

'Good for you, Margaret,' I said. Margaret was always a gentle girl, but I'd often felt there was a lot of pain and hurt pent up inside her. I could see us all now, standing together in the room off the kitchen – Margaret, Anne, Sissy, Kathleen McGarry – sweet, sad country girls, like most of the girls at St Joseph's. And us two tough little Dubliners. Bernadette and me.

Bernadette wasn't sweet or sad. She was thin with short black hair, and she had a way of suddenly looking at you, suspiciously, as if she was wondering whether you were thinking odd thoughts about her. A second later she would silently clench her fist at you. She did this to all the girls – in the classroom, in the laundry, even during Mass. Bernadette was always silently warning us not to think bad of her – or else! – up went that threatening fist.

When Bernadette wasn't clenching her fist at someone, she was chewing her nails – walking around chewing frantically as if she had a ton of stress on her thin, hunched-up shoulders. We'd been at St Joseph's for about six months when I finally discovered the reason for Bernadette's intense nail-chewing – she was planning her escape. She just hadn't worked out the when and how.

I was so excited I wanted to hug her. Trust another Dublin girl to have the same idea!

'I've escaped before,' I told her, 'from a Home in Dromcondra. I didn't get caught for two years, but I had to live in the park.'

Bernadette looked at me curiously. 'So how come you were caught again?'

'Yeah, well I got caught – but I didn't get caught for *two years*. And that was only because somebody told on me.'

Bernadette started chewing her nails furiously again, her face thoughtful. Finally she looked at me and nodded: 'All right, I'll let you in on this then. But you'd better not feck it up this time. And keep your mouth shut about it, do you hear?'

In the weeks that followed, whenever we got a chance we discussed our plans. We were two skinny kids from Dublin, but we spoke with the tough seriousness of two jailbirds who had spent years in Alcatraz.

On the night of our breakout Bernadette and I slipped out of bed and got dressed in slow and careful silence. The rest of the dormitory was asleep. The nuns were asleep. The whole building was in darkness. We sneaked across the dormitory floor and with every creak of a floorboard we stopped, petrified.

Once in the dining-hall downstairs we unlocked a window and slowly pushed it up. But we'd forgotten about the gravel path. After every crunching step we held our breath, eyes darting up to the windows, afraid a light would appear.

We grazed our knees as we clambered on to the outer wall. Bernadette jumped first, then I got over, using her bent and wavering shoulders as a stepladder.

Bernadette lost her balance and we both fell.

'That was a sloppy start!' she said accusingly.

'Don't be blaming me,' I said. 'You were the one that fell.'

'Come on, shurrup, let's get going.'

Like blade-runners, we charged into the darkness, chins thrust out and elbows back, *running, running*, as far away from St Joseph's as we could get. Finally we paused for breath. 'God,' I said, 'God Almighty, we did it, Bernie. We got away!'

It was nearly pitch-black, with only an eerie light from the half-moon. It seemed to be watching us, blinking ominously whenever a black cloud passed over it.

'Look at the moon, Bernie,' I said, 'doesn't it look like an eye?'

'No, it looks like a fucking banana.' And then Bernadette added quickly, 'Did you notice what I just said, Christina? About the moon?'

'About it looking like a banana?'

'No, I said a *fucking* banana! Isn't it great to be able to swear again!'

It was so dark, we had to stop and keep checking we were still walking on the road and not into the lake. Every so often the road narrowed and it felt as if the mountains were closing in to crush us. But we carried on, determined to reach Dublin. We were free, triumphant. We were on the run big-time now.

The fog over the lake seemed to make our low voices echo louder. We decided to have fun. Bernadette walked about five steps up the mountain and called out: 'C-H-R-I-S-T-I-N-AHHHHH! OOOOOH . . . OOOOOH!'

I called back. 'B-E-R-N-A-D-E-T-T-E, THE BANSHEE IS BEHIND YOUUUUUU!'

Bernadette screamed and ran down. She was terrified of the Irish banshee, the ghost of a woman with long black hair. 'Don't be coddin' me!' she spluttered. 'You're an awful eejit! That could have damaged me heart!'

Back on the road, we stopped joking and began to talk of our dreams of getting back to Dublin. Bernadette's dreams were of going home to her mother. All she really wanted was to see her mother again. 'Are you dying to see your mammy again, Bernadette?' I said.

'Yes,' she replied, 'because I have a fucking bone to pick with her!'

Galway, we knew, was fifty miles away, but if it had been a thousand miles we wouldn't have cared. We planned to reach it by seven o'clock in the morning, and we were going to board the Galway train to Dublin. If we couldn't board the train, we were going to walk the tracks all the way. Big-time. We were on the run big-time. We never stopped to think about what we were going to eat and drink on the way. It didn't even enter our heads. We were tough escaped jailbirds, we could do anything, get away with anything.

We marched on, two skinny little city girls, armed with our wild imaginings and our longing for Dublin. We talked of the white swans gliding on the murky green water of the Grand Canal. We remembered each bridge, and the barges on their way down to Carlow to pick up the sugar for Guinness's Brewery. The Connemara landscape was alien to us – nothing but mountains and lakes and just one long winding country road that led to Galway.

It seemed like we'd walked a thousand miles and still there was no sign of the place. The moon was disappearing and then it blacked out completely. The road narrowed again as it wound its way uphill between two mountains. Suddenly we heard a strange sound, like a man with heavy club feet walking slowly towards us.

'What's that . . . ?'

We stopped and grabbed each other. I could feel a sweat of terror breaking out on me. Bernadette began to shiver. We stood petrified as the leaden footsteps came closer in the darkness.

All at once the clouds shifted and the moon cast a bright shaft of light on the road before us, and we saw him – an ugly beast with a long manky face. Bernadette almost jumped out of her skin and screamed. 'Jesus God – it's the Devil himself!' We turned and ran like two terrified rabbits, back down the road.

When we reached the lake I was panting for breath and I

tried to grab Bernadette to stop her running, but she was unstoppable. We cleared the distance back to St Joseph's in half the time it had taken us to get away. When we reached the outer wall it was almost dawn. By now I'd realized what had happened out there, and I was livid.

I grabbed Bernadette's arms and shook her. 'You fool, you. That wasn't the Devil – it was a harmless old *donkey!*'

'A donkey . . . ?' Bernadette was looking at me in her old suspicious way again. 'Are you sure? . . . He looked a lot like the Devil to me, so he did.'

'Bernie, will you stop acting the eejit. If we turn around we can still make it. We could hide out in a farmer's barn somewhere and still get the train from Galway tomorrow morning.'

'Oh no! You're not getting me out there again!'

'But, Bernie, it's only a *donkey!*'

'No.' Bernadette shook her head positively and I could see the fear was still in her. 'Are you forgetting what the nuns are always telling us? About how the Devil can turn himself into a club-footed animal? Sure the Devil was in that donkey out there. It thought it would fool us.'

I stood looking at her, uncertain. It made sense in a way but I decided to keep this thought to myself. Bernadette acted like such a hard nut she might tell the others it was me who'd led the charge back.

Bernadette lifted her foot. 'Here, give us a hoosh up this wall and let's get back inside before we're missed.' I cupped her foot in my hands and gave her a push up the wall. At the top she sat astride and stretched a hand down to pull me up. Ten minutes later we were back in our beds, lying under the blankets with our long grey night-shifts over our day clothes. Just in time.

'Get up! Come on, get up!' Rubberbelly was in to wake us all up, whacking the beds with her long pole. I looked over at

Bernadette. She was very pale. I knew that in the cold light of day we were both thinking the same thing. Compared to our jailers the donkey on the mountain was probably a harmless old thing.

NINETEEN

T his was a city that lived in the present, and thank God for that I thought, as the taxi wove its way through the Saigon rush-hour. I'd had enough of spilling my guts out about the past.

Young Vietnamese businessmen zoomed past on their Hondas with their briefcases strapped behind them. Stunning girls wearing the traditional *ao dai*, the graceful silk tunic and trousers, with dark glasses and little straw hats, rode by on mopeds. I'd grown to love the elegance of the Vietnamese, their sense of fun and their zest for life. I loved the energy and the hectic buzz, the frantic honking of horns, the fact that everyone is always smiling.

But then there were the children. Saigon was still full of people who were trapped in its past.

Michael and Androula had generously offered to come and help at the Foundation for six months. They were both qualified social workers now, with a special interest in the care of disabled children. By the time I returned from Australia they had arrived and we all got together over a meal cooked by Nicolas and Sara. It was great to have the family around me in Vietnam. Children don't ask to be born and I'd never wanted mine to feel they owed me anything. But they'd come to me of their own free will, and there was such a strong love between us. We often argued fiercely, but I knew I could always count on them.

Bé was toddling now, and she and Nicolas were completely in love. Every day Bé would clamber up the stairs to the office to look for him and if he wasn't there she would look under all the tables and chairs. Then she would sit on the floor staring glumly around as if to say 'Where is he? Why isn't he here?'

If Nicolas didn't appear Bé would go over to his desk and sit under it until he came back. If he was too long she would cry and cry, and nothing we gave her would distract her. We'd try everything – wooden blocks, toys, bags of coloured sweets – but it was only Nicolas she wanted. If he was out at a meeting we'd often phone him and say: 'Bé's under your desk, so don't be too long.' He always said he missed many a good business opportunity because of Bé.

When she heard Nicolas's voice Bé would creep out from under the desk and look at him reproachfully, whimpering and stretching her arms out to him. He would pick her up and swing her round, then sit her on his lap while he got to work calmly on his computer. Nothing fazed Nicolas. He and Sara both loved children. There was always a toddler around the office, pulling boxes out and playing with the books, and it was rare to see either of them without a child in their arms or on their lap. I knew they had talked about adopting Bé. But they felt at this point that their own life was too insecure.

We were having a long hard fight for Bé because her mother wanted her back. I knew that if we gave her up she was as good as dead. There were terrible reasons why Bé shrank from women. Then a diplomatic couple who had already adopted one Vietnamese child came to the centre and fell in love with

Bé. We don't arrange adoptions at the Foundation, that has never been our philosophy, but Bé needed to be as far from Vietnam as possible, and eventually we obtained her mother's permission.

Nicolas and Sara were happy for Bé, but it was heartbreaking. The couple would often come in to play with her, or take her out, but if she spied Nicolas, she would immediately try to run to him. Nicolas did his best to keep out of the way. I think it was agony for both of them.

On the day Bé was leaving for America I said to Nicolas, 'Why don't you take the morning off and spend it with Bé?'

I could see he was on the verge of tears. 'I don't think I can bear to, Mom,' he said, 'it would break my heart. I'm sorry, I can't even say goodbye to her. If you don't mind, I think we'll go out.'

After lunch he and Sara came down and peeped through the window of the medical centre. Bé was there, all ready to go. She was wearing a new rainbow-coloured dress and a matching headband. She had on white frilly socks and little red strap shoes with a pom-pom on the side, and she had a little matching red string bag. She looked absolutely gorgeous.

Nico handed me a letter and a photograph. It was a picture of Nicolas and Sara and Bé on one of their outings to the park. The letter was addressed to Bé and was marked 'Private'. I could only guess at what was in it. 'Will you kiss Bé for me', Nicholas asked, 'and give her these? She can read the letter when she grows up.'

They took one last look at Bé in all her glory, making sure she didn't see them. Then Nicolas turned suddenly and he and Sara went out quickly and got on to his motor-bike. As they rode off I could see that they were both crying.

That night I wrote a poem as I sat thinking about Bé. I called it 'Little Heroine':

Born in the storm,
Tossed like a little bird with broken wings,
Fragile, left dying in the heap.
They dug deep into your soul, Bé.
Around you the blue thundering flashes showed no
    mercy.
Now you are free, Bé,
A beautiful wild rose
That blows in the free wind.
You are not of the storm, Bé,
You are freedom, you are joy.
The flame that was born within you never went out,
You are now a beautiful dove with strong wings.
One day you will wrap them around some other little
    birds with broken wings
And carry them to your nest.
Fly, Bé, fly. Stay free.
I will always love you. God bless you.

The long-term damage to children like Bé can be horrendous. With care and medical expertise we can nurse starved and abused children back to health but the emotional scars they have are deeper than the physical ones. One day, perhaps, Vietnam will have its own psychologists specially trained to help these children, but for the moment all we can do at the Centre is restore their bodies, and then support them with our love. I do believe that children can heal themselves on love, but sometimes they need more.

Many of the disabled children who come to the Centre have been rejected by their families. In Vietnam any kind of deformity is seen as a bad omen – possibly a curse placed by an angry outsider on the family. However beautiful the child and however slight the disability, it stands the risk of being abandoned. Travelling round the world, seeing parents loving and caring for their disabled children, I often think of the beautiful little broken birds who end up in our care, whose parents cannot love them or accept them.

With their special experience Androula and Michael helped us to help our disabled children, especially those who had cerebral palsy. They showed the staff how to turn eating and dressing into learning games. This helped the children over practical hurdles in a way that was fun, and it increased their confidence. With the resources we had we couldn't do more, but Michael and Androula's patient input helped us a great deal.

Towards the end of the year we had a visit from Henrietta Schaffer of the Schumacher Foundation in Holland. Nicolas went to fetch her from the airport and returned with a small, dynamic, forthright woman who seemed to understand immediately what we were about. Henrietta was interested in us at every level. She and Nicolas had many discussions about the workings and finances of the Foundation and I was touched when Nicolas told me Henrietta was concerned about my health. She left us on an upbeat note with dinner at the Continental Hotel. We felt she had become a real friend, but she made no promises.

It was time for the family to leave. Michael and Androula had work to return to in England, and Nico and Sara were going to Australia where Nico was planning to do a degree in criminology. I knew that I was going to miss them all very much.

A few days before Nico and Sara left a letter arrived from Henrietta Schaffer. The Schumacher Foundation would support the Medical and Social Centre financially 'for an indefinite period'. I couldn't believe it. I kept reading the letter over and over again. Then we threw our arms round one another and jumped and danced round the office, laughing and shouting. I ran down to the shop and got some Coca Cola to celebrate.

'Thank you, Henrietta! You've saved the Foundation! Thank you, God! Thank you, Nicolas,' I kept shouting. 'You're wonderful, you're fantastic, you're brilliant!'

So many good things were happening. We had some real financial security at last, and all around me I could see children growing, learning, getting jobs, realizing their dreams. The boys in the Shelter were doing well. Some of them had saved up the money they made from street-selling to buy themselves bikes. There was less fighting and swearing and stealing. Dung, a very tough little boy who had often been in knife fights when he was living on the streets, had even turned in some money he found to the staff.

We had a big ally in David Shortlands, the Laundry Manager at the Saigon Prince Hotel. He had given work to several of our boys, and was impressed by how eager and efficient they were. With the help of the Pfizer Company, Nga had realized her special dream. Nga had severe scoliosis, a painful condition of the spine. She had been living by selling postcards in the street, but she had always dreamed of working on a computer in an office, and she had taught herself to speak English fluently.

Now Pfizer's office in Vietnam had agreed to employ her, and the Foundation was helping her with private computer lessons.

Perhaps the best day of the year for all of us was 21 June, when Trung walked into my office. He was wearing leg braces and special shoes and he was walking with a stick, but he was walking on his own. His face, as he slowly but determinedly made his way across the room to me, was triumphant. He hadn't walked since he was three.

Trung went for intensive physiotherapy at our clinic in Phuan Nuang district. Gradually his legs and joints grew stronger, he became accustomed to the braces and shoes, and eventually he was even able to run, though not very fast. So one of Trung's dreams had come true. At the end of July he realized the other – he got a job with the post office in Vung Tau. It was an emotional moment for us all when Trung came to say goodbye. He had shown so much courage and I was sure he was going to be successful.

I have to admit that things with our teenagers weren't always so rosy. Some of them had been too damaged by their lives to have any real ambitions. All we could do was be there for them when they needed us and hope that one day, with our help, they would be able to change.

Lam was a case in point. I'd met Lam when he was sixteen, and by then he had been involved in the sex trade for several years, hiring himself out to foreign tourists and getting himself into all kinds of terrifying situations. He was a gentle boy, but he was always borrowing money and then having to borrow more at high interest from the street mafia to pay off the people he owed.

One night I had a distress call. Lam sounded petrified: 'Mama, please, you have to help me. I in big trouble. Mafia wait for me and hit me, hit me, hit me, long time, very hard.'

I went downtown to where Lam was waiting. He looked a wreck. He told me he owed the mafia $60 plus $140 interest, and they had given him till the next day to come up with the money. Lam had a deformed foot and the mafia thugs had repeatedly stamped on it till he couldn't walk. He said that if he didn't give them the money they would kill him.

'How many bloody times are we going to go through this,

Lam?' I asked, exasperated. 'How many times have I got to tell you to keep away from these people?' Because I'd been a street child myself I knew how to deal with shady characters, and the street mafia didn't intimidate me. I'd had many a run-in with them over the years. But I knew Lam was in real danger this time. I decided I'd have to pay them off myself.

'If I ever catch you hurting a child again I'll f——g kill you with my own bare hands,' I told the gang when I found them. They looked at me nonchalantly. They'd heard that from me before.

Unfortunately, Lam hadn't learned his lesson. He was still hanging out in bars and getting picked up by strangers. We'd encouraged him to go to school and we'd talked to him about the risks he was taking, but I had to face the fact that, for now anyway, we had failed.

Another of our children, Nam, had also got caught up with the mafia. Nam had been abandoned as a toddler in a park near the zoo, and he had survived there for a long time by begging from tourists, and by receiving the odd bowl of rice from local stallholders. But when he got older he realized he could make bigger money in Pham Ngu Lao, and that's where I'd come across him.

I often went down to the tourist areas at night to see how the kids were doing and to try and warn them about the dangers. I knew that a lot of them had only one thing to sell – themselves. It is hard for a street child to grasp the reality of HIV and AIDS. Usually I tried to persuade them to come to the Shelter, but with a lot of them I knew it was no good – the street was all they knew and that was where they felt they belonged.

Nam was a real scallywag and very smart. He'd picked up French and pidgin English and he had a cheeky confidence which I knew made him attractive. For a while I'd persuaded him to come to school, and we had even supplied him with a bike, which he sold almost immediately for a fraction of what it cost us. When he came to the office he danced round, giving the staff a perfect rendering of 'Hotel California' by the Eagles which blares out from every speaker in Saigon – another legacy from the Americans.

One night I was sitting in a coffee shop on Dong Khoi when another boy called Loi came running over to me. Loi was one of the older children in Pham Ngu Lao, and he and I got along well. He told me he had seen Nam getting into a car with two foreign men and later on he'd seen one of the street mafia giving Nam money. I'd known for a long time that Nam was having sexual encounters, but I thought he'd managed to steer clear of the street mafia.

I didn't see Nam for a week. Eventually I found him lurking behind a row of Hondas and asked him if he'd like to join me for a cold drink. I realized he'd been hiding from me because he knew that I knew what he had been up to. He looked at me cautiously.

'I'm not angry with you,' I said. 'You know me better than that.'

Nam wasn't giving much away but he did tell me he'd been turning tricks with the mafia for about two months. 'The longer you do it, the harder it'll be to get away,' I said. I knew Nam wouldn't come to the Shelter, but I had an idea. 'I need a night-time guard at Tu Xuong Street,' I said. 'Would you like to take it on?' Of course I didn't, especially not a fifteen-year-old, but it seemed the only way to get Nam off the streets.

Nam was thrilled. He turned up next night and while I cooked him some popcorn and hot dogs to make things seem nice and normal, he watched a video. When I came back he was curled up with one of our big teddy bears, just like a two-year-old. It nearly broke my heart. How can anyone abuse children like this? The bastards! But unfortunately Nam only lasted four days as a guard. The pull of the street was too much for him.

Nam didn't know when his birthday was, but we discovered that he had been born on 7 July, four days before my own son Nicolas. I told Nam it was a special time for me, and I'd like to give him a party. We chose the Banana Café, and I went down with a vanload of balloons and a big cake which said 'Happy Birthday Nam' in bright purple icing. All the street kids for miles around had got word of the party, and huge amounts of ice-cream, soft drinks and sweets disappeared in no time at all.

We were all having a great time when I noticed that Nam wasn't there. I went to look for him, and found him in an alley, crying his eyes out. I put my arms around him and after a while he told me that this was the best day of his life, and he just wished he had a family to go with it.

'Nam, why don't you come and live at the Shelter?' I asked.

'I don't want to live in your bloody Shelter,' Nam said, 'I want a family of my fuckin' own. Is it too much to fuckin' ask?'

TWENTY

I'D KNOWN Ha almost from the time I arrived in Saigon. He was ten when I first met him. He was a scrawny little street child, very small for his age, and he spent a lot of time hanging about by the Saigon River. When Ha was around you knew you had to watch your pockets.

He wasn't an attractive-looking little boy. His teeth were all on top of each other, like a crooked house, and his mouth always seemed to have saliva at the corners. Every few minutes he would suck air in audibly through his teeth. I knew what that meant. Ha had dental problems. But the first things I noticed were his hands. They weren't the hands of a ten-year-old boy, they were like a mechanic's hands, cut and rough, and his nails had eaten deep into the scabbed, peeling skin.

Ha had had no love in his life. He seemed to have no family. He'd been in and out of prison, and he'd developed a tough, macho manner, but inside he wasn't tough at all. I knew it would be hard to help him because he had a very low opinion of himself. We tried to persuade him to come to the Sunshine School, but he wasn't interested – he just wanted to have fun. I could see the road he was going down would lead him into trouble. He was already into drugs, and when he was twelve he went back to prison for theft.

I caught up with him again when he came out. He'd been in prison for two years, and all his swagger had gone. There had been tougher guys than him in there. His arms had been burned with cigarettes and there were deep scars all over his body. This time he came to see me and said: 'I like you help me, Mama Tina. I like go school.' Ha had made many promises to me in the past and hadn't kept them. I decided to wait. The staff in the office had already lost patience with him and told me not to waste my time.

A week or so later Dan phoned me. 'Ha's been up to the office again,' he said. 'I really do think you're wasting your time with this guy, Christina. He'll be back to his old self in a few weeks. We've got so many other kids to take care of, kids who really want to do well.'

'Well,' I said, 'you know there's always a black sheep in the family. It's usually the ones who've suffered most that need us most.'

Dan said, 'You never listen.'

'It's just as well,' I said. 'If I'd listened I'd never have come to Vietnam in the first place.'

I could almost hear Dan shrugging. 'Oh well, it's up to you.'

I called a meeting about Ha. Even the social workers thought I was wasting my time. 'I don't think we should be selective,' I insisted. 'I think we should love *all* children. I can't turn my back on him. It goes against my philosophy. Never say never. Isn't that what James Bond said?'

Helen Thuong said diplomatically, 'It doesn't mean we don't *want* to help him. But I've seen you try so many times and you are always disappointed.'

'No I'm not,' I said. 'I don't expect him to change over-night. After all, what's he got? He hasn't got any education –

only what he's learnt on the streets. But this is the first time he's ever asked for help.'

Helen smiled at me philosophically. 'That's why I love you, Mama Tina,' she said. 'You never give up.'

'Okay,' I said to Ha, 'we start again. But no bullshit. Okay?' He nodded. 'Okay.' There was a problem, however. The other kids in the Sunshine School looked up to him as a gang-leader. But Ha was illiterate. He'd have to start from scratch and then he would lose face. I decided to pay for him to have private lessons. This time Ha kept his promises. He turned up on time and worked hard.

Ha had never really told me anything about his family except that his father was dead. One night he phoned me and said, 'Mama Tina, I want talk with you alone. Can you meet me in café in Thanh Ha Ba Trung Street?'

Dan had invited the staff home for dinner. It was always a special occasion, and I'd had a long day. But somehow I knew this was important. When I phoned Dan and told him about Ha, I could hear his disapproval. 'Okay, Christina,' he said. 'Do what you have to do. I expect he's in trouble again.'

I took a Honda-om down to Thanh Ha Ba Trung Street. Ha was sitting on the pavement waiting for me. His face lit up in a crooked smile.

We went inside and sat down. 'Do you want a cup of tea?' I asked him.

'Coca.'

'That's not good for your stomach.'

'So why I see you 'rink Coca Cola, Mama?'

'Ah, that's only Coca Cola *Light*, no sugar.'

'Ohhh, but I 'rink same, same,' he grinned.

'So, what's the problem?' I asked, when we'd ordered.

Ha hesitated. Then he said, 'When my mama have me in the stomach, my papa die. When I very small boy, she marry

SUNSHINE

new man and have two boys. But her new man not love me.
So I go live on street.'

'Ah, now I understand,' I said.

Ha looked at me earnestly. 'Now I say you, Mama Tina. I
like go see my mama. I so happy if you help me see my mama.'

'Is it a long time since you saw your mama?' I asked him.

'So long time.'

'Where does she live?'

'Tu Thiem, across river, District 4. Mama very poor.'

'Do you want me to go and see her? Or do you want us to
go together?'

'I like we go same, same.'

Next morning we boarded the Colusa Ferry, a battered old
rust-bucket which goes back and forth across the river all day.
It's always packed solid with Hondas and people, and I was glad
the journey was only ten minutes – I wasn't sure which was
worse, crossing on the rust-bucket or swimming across in the
polluted water.

I knew Tu Thiem, a densely populated shanty town of
small wooden shacks hanging over the river. Sometimes,
during the monsoon rains, some of them would collapse into
the water. The river is used for everything in Tu Thiem,
washing, urinating and cleaning fruit and vegetables, and the
place was full of rats.

Many people knew me and greeted me from their doorways
as Ha and I walked down the narrow dirt track looking for his
mother's house. Suddenly he stopped and said, 'This my mama
house . . .' There was a little bit of wood to make a gate at the
entrance. 'I'll wait here,' I said.

Ha seemed very nervous. 'Surr Mama Tina stay here? Surr?'

'I won't go away,' I reassured him.

Eventually Ha called me in. The house had one room
which had a double bed, a box sideboard and a little area for a

155

wood fire. There was a photograph of a man on the sideboard. 'That my papa,' Ha said. 'He die.'

'You look like him,' I said.

His mother seemed a little embarrassed, but we managed to understand one another with Ha interpreting. I told her that Ha was doing well at school. I said the streets were dangerous, and suggested we find him a sponsor so that if he lived at home we could help to pay for his keep. I asked if she would bring the other two children to the Centre, and she seemed pleased. She said she would like to send them to school, but her husband made only just enough money for food by selling cigarettes on the street.

Ha walked me to the Colusa Ferry and travelled across the river with me, just to make sure I got back safely. 'Will your mother have you back?' I asked him. He nodded, and I noticed that for the first time he looked happy. From then on Ha's school work really took off, and he seemed gentler and more at ease with himself. One day Ha actually gave me a kiss on the cheek. I was stunned. I waited for him to ask me for something, but he didn't. It felt like a new beginning.

'Never say never,' I said to Dan.

TWENTY-ONE

IN THE SUMMER of 1996 Helen came to visit. She and I look so much alike that everywhere she went in Saigon she was besieged by children. Like me she is for ever singing, our house was always full of music, and before long she and the children were singing together – 'You are my Sunshine', 'We are the world.' The children loved Helen and she loved Vietnam. 'I'll be back, Mom. Before you know it I'll be back,' she said to me as she left, just as Nicolas had done. She was. Within six months she had put her career on hold and she was back in Tu Xuong Street.

For a long time she and I had been talking about setting up a music programme. I wanted the Sunshine children to have more than just the three Rs. Feeding a child's spirit and soul is just as important to me as health care or education. In the Sunshine School we had a little girl called Hanh, who at seven was already an exceptional artist. Hanh's mother was mentally ill and had abandoned her, and she lived in the slums in Nhieu Loc with her grandmother. But Hanh painted her dreams: detailed landscapes, houses, flower gardens and exotic animals in the most wonderful, brilliant colours. A sponsor was paying for Hanh to have private art lessons and her paintings were becoming stronger and more colourful still. She had even started getting commissions from people in the expatriate community and the money was going into a trust fund to help her go to art school.

Helen felt that for obvious economic reasons most of our support came from the expatriates in Saigon. The Vietnamese love music and she wanted to break down barriers with the music programme, so she approached the director of the famous Ho Chi Minh Conservatory. 'I've come from the other side of the world to give Vietnamese children music, so please help me,' she said. The director was impressed, and so was his daughter, Hoang Diep. Diep, who is a distinguished pianist and composer, offered to come and be our music teacher.

The Sunshine Music Club held its first meeting in May 1997. Thursday was the only day when there was a spare class-room, so the club met once a week. Some parents didn't want their children to come because they thought it would inter-fere with their work. 'If you get up early you won't be able to sell properly tonight,' they would tell them.

When a small child works till four or five in the morning and then creeps out before their parents are awake, you know they are keen, and sometimes ninety or a hundred children would turn up. No child was ever turned away, and if there were too many to fit inside, the class went out into the court-yard.

Diep started by teaching them Vietnamese songs, because most of them knew nothing about their own culture. Then they learned English songs with Helen. The keen ones learned to read music, and when the Sunshine Choir was launched even the families started getting interested. Helen encouraged them to come along, and often a mother or a sister or an uncle or an aunt would be seen shyly peering through the window.

Street children have wonderful voices and a natural sense of rhythm – everything that is sold on the streets of Saigon has its own special little signature tune which is beaten out on a sheet of metal with a metal stick or a hollow piece of wood. At first the club had only improvised instruments, but after a while Diep found a piano, and a school in Australia gave us some guitars. Les Blair was still a good friend to the Foundation. When he moved to work for British Gas he persuaded them to give us money to build on an extra classroom to the school, and then music classes went up to four a week.

Staff at the Saigon Prince Hotel had decided to help the school in a very practical way. Each month they presented two children with a bike each. A bike does everything for a family in Saigon and the bikes not only enabled the children to get to school but were also used to earn money, and to take the family out for the day.

Children could stay at the Sunshine School as long as they wanted, but if they wanted to go to mainstream school, we helped them. By this time we had six full-time teachers, and the children followed a proper curriculum and took exams, which meant that they could produce a certificate to prove that they had been educated up to a certain grade. Most of the boys in the Shelter went to local schools, and we also ran literacy classes in the study room at the top.

We had given the Shelter a facelift and it felt very homely. As a reward for their good behaviour I'd got the boys new pine bunks, and the sitting-room had been redecorated and provided with green and white rattan furniture. I encouraged the children to grow their own plants on the balcony. Even looking after a plant helps a child to develop some responsibility. There was a family atmosphere in the Shelter. Some children were there long-term, but we had managed to reunite several with their families. The oldest was seventeen, and he was so good with the younger ones I was thinking I might give him a job there.

But nothing was as important to the Shelter kids as the Sunshine Football Team which was already beginning to feature in Saigon's social pages. Some of the expatriates had begun taking the boys to play football at weekends in one of the parks and the children had become mad keen. Now they were training every Saturday in the local football stadium. They'd even got a special green and yellow 'Sunshine strip'. During 'British Week' Trevor Brooking, the West Ham player, had visited Saigon and the boys went to his coaching clinic. At the end of the week Trevor awarded them the trophy for the best junior team and presented them with a computer. The boys were over the moon. It was as exciting as the Cup Final at Wembley. They also had a training session with a French first-division team, and they were showered with free gifts from sports manufacturers.

Lap was still with us at the Centre. So many people had now met or heard about Lap from our newsletters that he had an international fan club, and we had enquiries from around the world about how he was getting on. He wheeled himself about the Centre, used the computer, and spent time with his good friend Quoc. But I still wondered what his future was going to be.

Then something wonderful happened for Lap. I was telephoned by a woman called Margaret Hunt, whose husband, Robert, was working in Vietnam. Margaret asked if she could come and help us.

'I'm a special needs teacher,' Margaret told me.

'Special needs?' I said. 'We're full of children with special needs here – all kinds of needs. How much love have you got? That's their biggest special need.'

Margaret had enough love and to spare for everyone, but as

soon as Lap and Margaret saw one another a real love affair began. From that moment Lap belonged to Margaret and Margaret belonged to Lap. With Margaret's help Lap mastered sign language and began to use his limbs more and to become more confident and independent.

When Robert and Margaret went home to Aberdeen they took Lap with them for a holiday, but when Lap reached Aberdeen he became ill. He was taken to see a specialist who suggested that he needed long-term medical treatment. The treatment was likely to take years, and after a great deal of thought Margaret and Robert decided they would apply to adopt Lap. The British government did everything possible to ease the way, and the process began to go ahead.

So Lap stayed on in Aberdeen, and with his new security he became a new person. Even his deafness was diagnosed as being less severe than we had thought. God, I thought, must have sent Margaret to this special child who needed so much extra love and attention. I had always prayed that Lap would find a family, and now, I knew, he had found the best family in the world.

Mongolia

TWENTY-TWO

This time it wasn't a dream, it was a word. It seemed to have come out of the air and it kept running through my head. Often it was there as I fell asleep. *Mongolia. Mongolia.* I didn't want to think about it, I was too busy. But Mongolia seemed to be calling me and that feeling wouldn't go away.

Someone asked me later whether there was any rational reason why I first went to Mongolia. No, I just had a feeling. It was quite different from other feelings, and for me it was reason enough. After all, a feeling like this had brought me to Vietnam.

In January 1997 I didn't even know where Mongolia was, just as I hadn't known where Vietnam was back in 1971. I didn't even know whether it was a separate country – I had a vague idea it might belong to China. But I asked Dan to find out whether there was such a thing as a Mongolian Embassy in Hanoi. There was. Dan and Helen teased me a little about it all, but they were used to my whims by now.

Then, as before, another signal came. 'Guess who's just been here?' said Helen Thuong when I came into the Centre one afternoon in April. 'David Pearson. And guess where he is working?'

'Where?' I said.

'Mongolia. He left you his number.'

David Pearson was a tall, charming Englishman who had been working in Vietnam and now, it turned out, was working with TACIS, a European Union educational group, in the Mongolian capital, Ulaanbaatar. Eventually, after some difficulty, I got him on the line.

'I'm coming to visit,' I told him.

'What are you actually going to do here?' asked David.

'Oh come on,' I said. 'You know me. What do I usually do?'

'Well,' David said, 'they've certainly got problems with the children here if that's what you mean. When are you coming?'

'The day after tomorrow,' I said.

Armed with a booklet on Mongolia I flew to Beijing where I was to spend the night – there were only three flights a week to Ulaanbaatar.

Beijing Airport was exhausting. I'd got myself a visa for Mongolia, but I hadn't imagined I needed one for China – after all, I reasoned, I was only passing through. At every gate there were hatchet-faced officials. It seemed I did need a visa, and I must also pay a hefty airport tax. No one spoke English. The only words we had in common were 'Visa' and 'Tax' which they spat at me like bullets.

After what seemed like a lifetime of getting lost in corridors and walking up and down stairs, I managed to get the necessary document and it was stamped by a tall, good-looking Chinese official who even managed a smile when, from sheer relief, I broke into a snatch of Irish song.

A bit shaken, and a lot poorer, I took a taxi to a small, drab hotel among the alleyways off the city centre, and then went out to explore. Beijing astonished me. I had no idea it would be so rich or so Westernized – full of luxury hotels and expensive cars. Off the wide boulevards I found restaurants of every nationality – German, English, Mexican, Russian, even a branch of the famous Paris Maxim's. I looked at the menu outside. *Sacré bleu!* – a dinner for two at Maxim's could only be mine if I won the Lotto! I returned to my hotel.

In my room I tried the television. It didn't work. Perhaps a nice shower, I thought. I tried the hot tap and the top came off in my hand. When I eventually managed to turn the water on, the shower fitment fell on my head. I thought about trying to call reception, but decided that even if they were willing to fix it, I was too tired to sit through a lengthy plumbing job.

I went to bed and tossed and turned on the lumpy mattress. Through the window of my darkened room I could see the neon outline of one of Beijing's big hotels flashing its message from the haves to the have-nots. Next morning I ate breakfast – a cup of tepid dishwater called tea and a piece of bullet-hard coconut cake – and took a taxi to the airport. Clearly Beijing had everything to offer that money could buy, but you certainly needed money to buy it.

I had been warned about MIAT, the Mongolian national airline. MIAT, I'd been told, stood for 'Maybe I'll Arrive Today', or possibly even 'Maybe I'll Arrive Tomorrow'. In fact the service seemed impeccable – comfortable, on time and manned by smiling cabin staff. The sky when we rose above the cloud carpet was a deep azure and as the plane banked and turned, a shaft of sunlight struck through the window and warmed my face. Below me I could see the great golden stretches of the Gobi Desert, and soon we were flying over vast plains dotted with great mountains. Everything seemed to be on a enormous scale.

I turned to my booklet. I learned that after seventy years of Soviet rule, Mongolia was now independent and penniless. Without subsidies from the USSR the Mongolian economy had crashed on a scale far worse than the Great Depression in the United States. Mongolian men who had been trained in Russia as technicians or engineers were now jobless or struggling as subsistence farmers. Many people were starving and alcoholism was rife.

I also learned another significant fact. Nearly one-third of Mongolia's population lived in the capital, Ulaanbaatar, and 40 per cent of these were under fourteen years of age.

Surprisingly, Ulaanbaatar Airport, though tiny, looked new and smart. I was fascinated by the appearance of the Mongolians. I had always imagined them to be squat and fierce, as I'd imagined Genghis Khan, but many were tall, golden-skinned and extraordinarily good-looking, and they all had the most ravishing smiles. Some had the true narrow Tartar eyes, but some looked far more Western – clearly the Soviet years had left their mark.

I could see David's tall, dark figure waiting by passport control. He was as friendly and welcoming as he had always been but I knew immediately that he was under pressure. As he drove me in the TACIS jeep along roads lined with grim Soviet-style buildings, he explained that life in a humanitarian organization in Ulaanbaatar was difficult, and he had a busy office to run.

David had booked me into a small, family-run hotel. 'Okay,' I said bravely, when he had seen me to the reception desk in the down-at-heel building. 'I'll be fine now. Don't you wait around.' The place smelled strongly of cooked mutton. As I soon discovered, it's a smell that permeates the air in Mongolia. Inside and outside, it gets up your nose, in your clothes and in your hair. Mutton and flour are the staple diet of Mongolian families, and over and over I saw café menus offering *buuz*, steamed mutton dumplings, and *horshor*, mutton dumplings deep fried.

A very thin young girl appeared to carry my suitcase, but I

couldn't bear to give it to her, she looked too frail and skinny. She led me upstairs to a coffin-sized room which contained a narrow metal bed on which there lay a hairy, rock-hard mattress covered in a yak skin, and a sheet and blankets. The yak skin sent me into fits of sneezing. The room was scorching. An antiquated Russian radiator clanked and gurgled in one corner. I threw open the window and looked out.

What I saw was extraordinary. The urban road, with its ramshackle wood and concrete buildings, led straight out on to the plain. I realized that even with all the high concrete blocks and squares added during the Soviet occupation, the ancient city of Ulaanbaatar was still tiny – an encampment in the middle of a vast steppe. In the distance I could see a great snow-covered mountain range, and at its foot what looked like a cluster of very large tents. These, I later discovered, were *gers*, in which the majority of the Mongolian people still live – I had seen them dotted across the plain as we drove from the airport. I was looking at a nomadic *ger* village.

As soon as I went out into the streets I felt at home in Ulaanbaatar. It reminded me of Ireland – not the Ireland of today, but the Ireland of my childhood. The women I saw talking on street corners or taking shortcuts through the back alleys reminded me of the women I'd known as a child back in the forties and fifties in the Liberties. They had the same scarves tied under their chins, the same way of carrying their old-fashioned shopping bags, the same bunched-up and belted coats and sturdy boots.

Like Ireland, Mongolia is a country of mountains and horses. Groups of booted horsemen wearing traditional *dells*, long orange and yellow coats with sashes, walked through the streets. I saw one of them vault quickly on to his horse and the animal didn't flinch, as if it and the man were one. I felt how cruel it must have been for these people, so connected to the land, to have been servants for so long to Moscow, their culture destroyed, their way of life suppressed. In parts of the city I came across the sad remains of ancient Buddhist temples. I knew I was in an oppressed country and it reminded me of my own.

Next day, through David, I met an American Peace Corps worker, Mark Zober, who asked if I would talk about my work to the Ulaanbaatar Rotary Club. The audience in the long dining-room of Ulaanbaatar's largest, indeed only real hotel, was a mix of Western businessmen and Mongolian professional people, and they listened to me attentively. In the silence that usually follows my talks, a distinguished-looking man with a mass of curly, slightly greying black hair came up to me. He was wearing a worn white shirt, a red cravat, a pin-striped suit and very old running shoes. Tears were running down his face. He told me, in elegant English, that his name was Boshigtt, and that he was vice-president of the Rotary Club.

Dr Boshigtt, I learned, had been a cardiologist, but his life under the Soviets had changed and he had become involved in politics. Now, he told me, he was deeply concerned about the children in Ulaanbaatar. Crowds of them came into the city from the countryside on the trains and ended up living rough, begging and stealing, and becoming involved in prostitution.

To keep warm they slept in the sewers, but in winter the temperature in Mongolia drops to minus 30°C, and many died from hypothermia and frostbite. During the Soviet regime, society in Mongolia had broken down. Incest was now common. Russian soldiers had raped women in the *ger* villages, and many children were born with gonorrhoea or syphilis. Often they were picked up for stealing or prostitution and ended up at the police detention centre pending a deci-

sion about what to do with them, or in prison, separated for
ever from their families.

As Dr Boshigtt spoke to me his eyes often filled with tears.
Though I was quite unable to pronounce his name, I knew
that he and I spoke the same language, the language of the
heart.

'Could you take me to see the children?' I said.

TWENTY-THREE

THE POLICE DETENTION centre to which Dr Boshigtt took me was a shack in a neglected-looking backyard – most of Ulaanbaatar looked like this I soon discovered. The centre was built of concrete and bits of old wood, put together in a rather random fashion. To the left of it stood a biggish concrete building and Dr Boshigtt told me this had once been some sort of children's clinic, but that it was now empty. I sensed it was something he didn't want to talk about too much.

There was something about his reluctance that made me ask to see inside, but once Dr Boshigtt had pushed open the main door, the building scared the hell out of me. It had the atmosphere of some kind of mental home or bedlam left over from another century. We walked down long, dirty, lost corridors with doors on either side. You felt you didn't want to know what was behind them.

At the end of one corridor there was a door slightly to one side, not immediately obvious. I had the feeling that behind that door was a place of solitary confinement where children had been put for punishment. I began to feel really bad. My imagination conjured up terrifying images of doctors with syringes, and I was back in the white-tiled room at St Joseph's, being stripped of all my clothes. I have no idea what really went on in that building, but my sixth sense told me that it was something terrible. It was harsh, like a punishment block, with ugly cracked tiles everywhere, and I couldn't wait to get out.

We walked the few yards to the detention centre and entered the office. Police in Russian-style uniforms with large caps and big boots were sitting idly around in front of a television set. There was also a cassette-player and it crossed my mind that these might have been donated for the children. Dr Boshigtt spoke with the officers in Mongolian, and the longer they talked the angrier he got. He began to raise his voice. I gathered we were being refused admission. 'How can they expect us to take care of our children if they won't let people help?' Dr Boshigtt said, turning to me furiously. 'The situation is disgraceful. We have to do something, not hide it.'

Eventually Dr Boshigtt won his point and one of the policemen got up and led us first into a shabby sitting-room where we waited for a while, and then into a long corridor. On the right was a door with peeling paint inside which I glimpsed some rough-looking showers, and to the left was a row of cell doors. The officer was hurrying us past, but I peered through the hatch in one of them, though I don't think I was supposed to.

At first all I could see in the dimness was a white mass, but after a second or two I realized that it was a kind of pyramid of children, piled one on top of the other in the tiny cell. Most of them were naked, though a few had bits of cloth or thin blanket wrapped around them. The children's heads were shaved and covered in scabs. It was hard to see which limb belonged to which child, but I could see that many of the legs and arms were covered in ulcers and bad, unhealed cuts.

Expressionless eyes gazed out at me. It was cold, bitterly cold. I looked at Dr Boshigtt but neither of us could speak.

I tried to push the door. It was locked, and the guard was signalling us to follow him. Further down the corridor he opened the door of a small room and motioned us inside. There was barely room for us to stand inside the room because it was packed with about fifty or sixty more young children, boys and girls sitting naked on the floor. There was a large television set in the corner which I sensed had been put there for my benefit since none of the kids was watching it. Apart from the mass of children the room was totally bare and freezing.

The children shuffled up a little to make room for me to sit down on the floor. They gazed at me, mostly in complete bewilderment. I put out my hand to the little girl nearest me – I never take a child's hand, I don't feel I have the right, I always give the child the choice. After a while she took it and I held it and chafed it. It was blue with cold. I felt utterly help-less.

The police officer was motioning to us again to follow him. Out in the corridor the little boys and girls from the cells were lining up outside the shower. They were aged about six to twelve I should say, and they stood there shivering and naked. One little girl was obviously dying, and was trying to stand up by leaning against the wall, but she kept slipping down it. Dr Boshigtt told me she probably had syphilis. One little boy had lost the toes on one foot from frostbite, another had lost half his leg and the wound was badly ulcerated. We were told that he had been thrown off a moving train and had lost half his leg on the track.

I held out my hands to the children. One little chap walked over to me and then the others gradually began to come. They stood beside me in the corridor and I put my arms around their shivering bodies. Dr Boshigtt just stood and watched with tears running down his face, which he didn't attempt to wipe away.

There was a doctor in the detention centre, and we asked to speak to her. I was glad there was a doctor, though I soon realized there was very little she could do to help. Dr Enhnaa explained to me through Dr Boshigtt that when the children were brought into the centre they were covered in lice, and so it was necessary to shave their heads and burn their clothes. That was why they were naked, though eventually they were given some kind of rough sacks to wear. She told me that a great many children had syphilis or gonorrhoea. 'We don't have the medicine to treat them,' she said. 'They need proper nourishing food, but we don't have it.'

Though what I had seen had shocked me inexpressibly, I felt that Dr Enhnaa was in fact a good person and genuinely concerned. She wasn't trying to hide anything, and this was something that I came to respect about the Mongolians. I've had too much experience of institutions not to know when people are putting on a show, and this woman wasn't. I found this everywhere I went in Mongolia, and because of this I somehow felt there was hope. The Mongolians had allowed me in and had let me see things the way they were. I respected them very much for that.

Dr Boshigtt and I stood outside the detention centre, and we were both crying. 'What do you think about the way the world treats children?' I said to him eventually. 'Allowing them to live and die without protection, without their basic human rights. Why do you think the world is like it is?'

For a while Dr Boshigtt didn't speak. Then he said, very sadly, 'You know we are very, very poor. We have nothing here – only mutton and horses. This country is landlocked between two great powers. We have no port and so we can't be independent – we have to trust to Russia and China to allow things through. The Russians took so much away from us. We don't even have the money to work our own mines, we have to let foreigners do it.

'Things are so bad in the countryside that people are gradually being wiped out,' Dr Boshigtt went on. 'We're such a small country, and if our children die, there will be nobody left. It's breaking our hearts. We don't know what is going to happen to us.'

We stood for a moment. I didn't know what to say. I kept thinking to myself: 'We're such a small foundation, and I'm struggling enough in Vietnam. If I do something here I'll have this to worry about too, and I'm worried enough already. Please God, just tell me what to do.'

Dr Boshigtt looked back at the grim concrete building. 'Do you think you could use that building to do something for the children?' he asked me. I shook my head vehemently. 'That place is a nightmare,' I said. 'It has so much pain in it. I feel it so strongly.'

'You're right,' said Dr Boshigtt.

I had rented a car and a driver to take me around Ulaanbaatar, and now I said to Dr Boshigtt, 'Can we drive out to that mountain over there? Will you come with me?'

The car drove us out across the great plain, and on either side I could see the encampments of the villages, with their clusters of great round tents. Near the foot of the mountain the driver stopped. The sheer space was breathtaking – literally – we were at such a high altitude I was finding it quite difficult to breathe. But just to be out of that oppressive city and that terrible building was wonderful. We got out of the car and stood in the breeze blowing across the plain. It was spring, and it felt so fresh, it was beautiful.

Suddenly everything seemed clear and obvious. 'I'd like to

build a village for the children, like these other ones,' I said to Dr Boshigtt, 'a small *ger* village.'

'Yes?' said Dr Boshigtt.

'We could start out with some education for the children,' I said. 'That's always a good way to begin, and we could have a little clinic in there for them. Do you think that makes sense? I don't know anything about your country and you don't know me either. But I just have the feeling I've got to do this, whether it's right or wrong. What do you think?'

Dr Boshigtt considered. Then he said, 'I think it is a very good idea.'

During the next few days I made a round of visits with Dr Boshigtt, including one to the President's Foreign Policy Adviser Dr Erdenchulun, a deep and spiritual man who was truly concerned about the fate of Mongolia's children. Dr Erdenchulun listened to me with great attention. He offered me his co-operation and we agreed that we would set up a study to investigate the situation and consider the feasibility of my plan. I knew I must start soon if I was to help the children before the savage Mongolian winter set in.

At the airport Dr Boshigtt and I said goodbye. 'You will return?' he asked, uncertainly.

I looked at him, this fine distinguished man in his worn suit and his ancient running shoes. 'Dr Boshigtt, never fear, I *will* come back,' I said. As Dr Boshigtt clasped my hand I knew that, in the short time I'd been there, Mongolia had etched itself upon my heart. I'd reached a point of no return, as I once had in Vietnam. There couldn't be any going back now.

TWENTY-FOUR

OUR STUDY OF life among Mongolia's poorest children produced a grim picture. The economic crisis and years of Soviet rule had destroyed Mongolia's traditional family patterns. School attendance was at an all-time low and children were running away from home to escape violence, which was often caused by alcohol, and sexual abuse. All over the countryside people were dying from starvation, and many children were now orphans.

Those who ended up on the streets of the three main cities had organized themselves into gangs and were surviving through prostitution and petty crime. The gangs were like families, working the streets during the day and sleeping in the sewers at night. Each gang had a leader who was effectively the parent, and the members of the gang would steal food and bring it back to be shared among the others. Children who were not in a gang had little chance of survival, and most said they would rather be in prison than on the streets. All of them were at risk from starvation, disease and the growing international sex trade.

When I read the report I thought long and hard. I wanted

to do something to help the children that would respect their traditional way of life rather than replace it – something that the Mongolians could develop themselves when the time and the economics were right. Another great need and an important task would be to try to unite children with their families and to give the families support. My new friends and contacts in Ulaanbaatar favoured the idea of a children's village. We all felt that from this small beginning other things might grow.

As always, the main problem was finding the money, and I spent many sleepless nights when I returned to Vietnam thinking about what I was taking on. I decided I'd have to return to Europe to fund-raise. Then, providentially, an Australian television producer who was making a documentary about the Foundation proposed flying me to Ireland. In less than a month I was on a plane.

I truly felt that God was watching over me on this trip. First, a man who had already been a great support to the Foundation gave me a huge donation for the Mongolian project. I would love to thank this man publicly, but he doesn't want to be thanked. His childhood in Ireland was as poverty-stricken as mine and though he is now very rich he has never forgotten what it is to be poor. I can only thank God for his generosity.

Secondly, I met a person who was to become very important to all of us, Una Henry. I had been asked to give a talk at St Anne's Church of Ireland church in Dublin – the Catholic Church in Ireland, I may say, has never invited me. Una had been brought along by another very special person, Barbara Donnelly, who knew of me because she had read my book. Afterwards Barbara discussed with Una the possibility of establishing an office for the Foundation in Ireland. After giving the matter serious thought and doing her homework on the Foundation, Una agreed to help.

Una is Director of Treasury at the Bank of Ireland and, as I was to learn, this behaviour was very typical of her – she stands back and considers before she does things, but when she's decided to do them she does them one hundred per cent. It was a marvellous moment when I met these two capable and committed women and learned that I had their support.

The third gift that came to me on this trip was my meeting with Wendy Evans. On my way back to Vietnam I stopped in England to speak at various churches in the Birmingham diocese and Wendy, as the Archbishop's personal assistant, turned up to drive me around. My first impression was of a small, neat woman with short grey hair – the kind of person the boss likes because she always has everything, including herself, under control. Then Wendy opened her mouth and a wonderful rich Brummy voice and a big hearty laugh came out. In the few days I was in Birmingham I grew to love Wendy, as well as the congregations she took me to meet. There was so much warmth and humour there, so much obstinacy and earthy humanity, that I immediately felt at home.

Wendy, I discovered, had recently been through a crisis in her own life. She had faced a serious illness and had recovered, and now she wanted to give something back. 'When I read your book,' she told me, 'I just knew that somehow, some day, I'd work for you. I'd like to take time off and help you for a year, if you'll have me.'

Would I have her! In August 1997 Wendy left for Mongolia and from then on she took over, fitting in with the country as if she'd been there all her life. There's only one Wendy, but how I'd love to clone her! From the start she was working eighteen hours a day without a break, meeting officials and social workers, overseeing the plans for the building of the village, and sending me letters and minutes of meetings that told me in every last detail what was going on.

The first step was to find a piece of land and we were offered several. Most of them were no good because they were subject to serious flooding – a hazard all over Mongolia because of the hills and mountains – or they were too expensive. But eventually we found a piece on the outskirts of Ulaanbaatar. There was a possibility that it might flood, but it was reasonably priced, and if there was a flood we would have three or four days' warning, so we decided to take our chances. That's one great advantage of *gers*, you can pick them up and move them.

By the time I arrived again in the summer we had acquired a flat in one of the high-rise apartment blocks to serve as a base, and the *ger* village was beginning to take shape within its circular wooden fencing. As I walked around it I felt I'd like to move in – a *ger* is the cosiest form of housing imaginable. It sits on a carefully laid wooden floor and is made of canvas thickly padded with waterproof material and layers of camel hair, all stretched over large poles which lean in to a central support. It has a dome at the top with a window to give light, a pipe to carry away the smoke from the wood-burning stove, and a wooden front door which usually faces south.

I had bunk beds made for the children with red, blue and yellow Mongolian designs on the sides, and little red and blue chests of drawers and wardrobes, with a place for them to keep their satchels and their schoolbooks. There were to be six residential *gers* each with room for seven people – six children and a Mongolian foster-mother, perhaps a woman who was homeless and jobless or who needed a refuge for herself and her child. There was a big communal *ger* which would be used as a classroom, one for the clinic and one for an office, where the security guard would sleep – I had been warned that life in Mongolia is dangerous, to say the very least.

I wanted the *ger* village to be a real village community, with each little unit living exactly as if they were at home, cooking and cleaning for themselves. The children would either go to school in Ulaanbaatar or attend classes in the *ger* village, where they could catch up with their education before going on to mainstream school. I also had visions of a communal kitchen where everyone could meet for meals, or entertain friends and visitors – a place where people of different nationalities could sit down together to eat and find out more about one another's lives. And I had dreams of converting an old building on the site into a greenhouse where the children could learn to grow vegetables and care for livestock.

There is such beauty and economy about a *ger* village, and nothing in ours was wasted. When a forty-foot metal container arrived with medicines and clothing from Ireland the builders transformed it into a shower and toilet block, with a laundry area and storeroom – an idea which greatly appealed to the children when they moved in. Sanitation in *ger* villages is normally primitive, and water is collected in large containers from the local pump.

We had already begun recruiting Mongolian staff and were getting together a very caring and professional team of counsellors, teachers and social workers. We also had the help of two Irish volunteers, and to our great delight Dr Boshigtt's daughter Ula had decided to join the team.

The Mongolian winter was beginning to close in. One icy afternoon I went with Dr Boshigtt and Nara, our Mongolian interpreter, to visit the children's prisons. It was a desolating experience. At the boys' prison, a grim building behind the main prison block, some of the ninety children were allowed out into the prison yard to speak to us. They stood there shivering and purple with cold as the wind whistled through their thin clothes. Some of them looked no older than six and most told us that they had been picked up for stealing because they had no other way of getting food. Most of them seemed to have lost touch with their families or had no relatives that they knew of. One little boy was deaf and mute and stood gazing sadly at us, looking completely lost.

Another little boy, Munkhbat, told us that his father had died of cancer three years previously and his mother had had to have a leg amputated not long afterwards. She had to crawl on all fours, Munkhbat told us, because a crutch was too expensive for her to buy. They lived on about $11 a month, and during the winter Munkhbat's younger brothers and sisters stayed at home because their clothes were not warm enough for them to go out. One day in July Munkhbat had stolen some clothing, and now he was in prison for three years. I sensed something terribly tragic in Munkhbat, and I felt I just had to try to do something to help him. In fact I wanted to open the prison gates and get all these children out.

'Do they get any kind of education here?' I asked Dr Boshigtt, and he shook his head. Some, he told me, worked in the prison bakery and the prison greenhouse, but they never tasted the vegetables they grew.

My visit to the girls' prison was more disturbing still. Like the boys' prison it was a stone building at the back of the main women's prison, though cut off and quite separate. This time we were allowed to pass the guards and go inside to meet the Deputy Warden, a large man in his fifties with a rugged red face and a thick Russian-style uniform.

He escorted us to the cells, and I was struck by the stark echoing emptiness of the stone-walled corridors along which we walked. The building was as desolate as a mortuary, and freezing cold. The Warden opened a cell door – four concrete walls, two metal beds and a bucket, and still this terrible fright-ening silence. Two young girls were huddled together on one of the beds. In their skimpy clothes they were shivering, and their lips were purple. Their poor little bodies looked pale and exposed, like two tiny chickens in a deep freeze.

I looked into their eyes, and I don't think, in all my life, I have seen such naked fear. I wondered what had taught them to be so terrified by the sound of footsteps approaching the cell door. Nara spoke softly with the older of the two, a stunningly lovely girl of about fifteen, slim, with raven black hair, black eyes and a beautiful, beautiful face. Every movement she made, every gesture of her hands, told me she was a born dancer. I could see her as a swan in *Swan Lake*.

She told us that her name was Armangul. She was not Mongolian but Cossack, and she had been trained as a ballet dancer from the moment she could walk. Both her parents had been teachers in Russia. Somehow, in the chaotic breakdown of the Soviet Union, Armangul had become separated from them – how this had happened or how she had come to be in Mongolia was not entirely clear.

Alone and frightened and hungry, Armangul had entered a *ger* house and taken some food from a cooking pan. While she was doing this the young daughter of the house had walked in. Armangul had panicked and thrown the pan at the girl, hoping to scare her away while she escaped. But the pan had hit the girl's skull and fatally injured her. Now Armangul was serving a life sentence for murder.

When Armangul had told us her story, Nara and Dr Boshigtt and I looked at one another helplessly. What could we do? I decided that one practical thing would be to get the girls some warmer clothes, and with the Warden's permission we drove to the market. Skimpily clad little children, blue with cold like all the others I'd seen, were heaving heavy sacks about, and for a moment I had a fantasy of building a huge fire somewhere and gathering them all around for a big plate of hot food. But 'One step at a time, Christina,' I reminded myself, and with Nara's help I found two coats, some thick sweaters and skirts, and two pairs of fur-lined boots among the various stalls. Imagining the long empty days in the prison cell, I also bought some pencils and paper, and when I saw a small television set for sale I scooped that up too.

When we returned to the prison I helped the girls to put the clothes on – their fingers were stiff with cold and I had to do up the buttons for them. We put the television set on one of the beds, hoping that somehow they would be allowed to watch it, but looking at the guard who was hanging about outside the cell I wasn't hopeful. I felt it was more likely he would take it and use it himself.

As I helped the girls I could feel the guard's eyes on my back, and when he stepped inside the cell I could feel their thin bodies contracting and shrinking away. I didn't want to think what their obvious terror of him meant. I could only show them with my eyes and my body that I intended to try to protect them from now on. I put myself between them and the guard, and I held them.

The guard was indicating that it was time to go. Up to that point the two girls had been more or less silent, but as we left Armangul looked at me and whispered something to Nara.

'What did she say?' I asked Nara.

'She is asking you "please come back",' Nara said.

TWENTY-FIVE

Together, straining, Nara and I lifted the heavy manhole cover. The night was black, and below me, too, I could see only blackness. I peered downwards. After a few minutes I could make out an iron ladder. I didn't want to go down it, but somehow I knew I must.

Nara went first. I put my hands firmly on the edge of the manhole, and lowered myself down, gingerly feeling for a rung with my foot. I was heavily wrapped up against the icy cold, and I didn't want to trip or catch my clothing. Holding the sides of the ladder tightly I descended somewhat shakily. The air felt dank but it gradually became warmer and then extremely hot. The ladder seemed to go on and on, but eventually I became aware that there was light.

The section of ladder ended and I realized that I was in a vast tunnel, lit by a few flickering candles dotted here and there. By my foot there was a sweet paper, the first little tell-tale sign that there were children around. A few feet away some kind of fizzy drink bottle was lying on the ground. Below us, in a black ditch, mysterious shapes were floating. There was a sodden Sainsbury's carrier bag – Sainsbury's bags seemed to be

186

a feature of Ulaanbaatar – an old shoe, and something nasty that I thought must be a dead rat.

Along the sides of the tunnel I could make out massive pipes. These, Nara had explained to me, belonged to the system installed by the Russians to provide constant hot water in the city. The pipes seemed to bulge into strange shapes, and these shapes began to move. They were children, lying one above the other on the warm pipes, as if they were in bunks. In the flickering light of the candles they climbed down to meet us. Like all the street children I'd seen they were dressed in an assortment of dirty, skimpy clothes. There were four little girls, two of them twins of about eleven or twelve who were wearing only tiny skirts and T-shirts. Nara spoke to them – she had been down to the sewers before with Caroline, one of our volunteers, and already knew some of the children.

There was a little collection of sticks and a pile of ashes, and some reddish fur. I pointed it out to Nara and she nodded. 'They cook down here,' she said. 'What do they cook?' I asked. Nara shrugged. 'A fox I think sometimes, if they find it.'

Nara told me that all these children belonged to one gang. The twins and one of the two older girls were sisters. They had been on the streets and sleeping down in the sewers for several years and had become very hardened. They acted as pimps for younger children, sending them into the park to pick up men. Mostly they would try to rob clients and do a runner before anything happened. Nara told me that to get into the gangs kids usually had to prove themselves by stealing, and there was some kind of initiation, which she thought was often sexual.

I looked at the four girls as they talked to Nara. I tried to imagine what they would have been like if they had been per-mitted to have a childhood. Even in that light I could see that the oldest one was a true beauty, with slanting eyes, high cheek bones and a proud, dignified face. Just for a moment I could see her dressed like a little English public-school girl, with a straw boater on her long black hair. She would have looked like a princess.

'I can't leave them here,' I said to Nara. 'Ask them if they'd like to come back to the apartment.' Nara looked at me for a moment as if she couldn't quite believe what I was saying, then she spoke rapidly to the children. They followed us back to the ladder and climbed up after us, out of the warm hell they called their home and into the freezing night.

The apartment block where we had our rented flat was a gaunt building faced with crumbling pebbledash, its concrete balconies breaking away in fragments. To me the whole of Ulaanbaatar felt as if it was crumbling to the ground. There was no lift and we walked up the six or eight flights of concrete stairs. Joan, another of our volunteers, opened the door, and the girls just stood on the threshold, not sure whether they were really being invited in. I sensed that they were on the lookout for a trap. I held the door wide open, and smiled a welcome, and eventually they stepped inside.

Joan, who had once been a cookery teacher, had made supper, and the children ate ravenously – I remember we ate roast beef and vegetables, an unusual treat for anyone in Ulaanbaatar. Then we bedded the four of them down on cushions from the sofa and, like any children, they fell asleep.

I was due to return to Vietnam at the end of the week, and I kept the girls with me until I left. I couldn't allow them back to the sewers, I simply couldn't, and I began negotiations to see if we could get them into the village, or at least to see if we could locate their families. In the meantime we took them down to the market and bought them decent jumpers and dresses and shoes, and navy jackets with hoods, and laced boots and good socks.

One evening I found them standing by the window, gazing out, and I saw that not far away a fair had been set up, with a huge colourful wheel which was turning, turning. It took me back to a night in the Sacred Heart orphanage in Dublin when, like them, I'd looked out and seen a fair in the distance and longed to go. 'Do you want to go?' I asked them through Nara. They were terribly excited. I gave them two dollars each, and for a moment their faces cleared and they looked like children again.

It didn't last long, however. They picked up some boys at the fair who had got hold of a bottle of vodka, and when they came back one of the twins was violently sick. 'Well, that's how it goes,' I told them. By now we had a kind of closeness, and they knew that, with me, there were some limits about how far they could go.

Through Nara the three sisters told me that they had been living on the streets for four years. They had left home when their mother had married a drunken, abusive man who used to beat them all up. One of the twins, Delga, I found particularly disturbing. She would sit on a chair, rocking and sucking her thumb as the tears spilled silently down her face. I would sit with her quietly, and eventually she allowed me to hold her hand.

It was no good asking her why she was crying. Her sadness was too deep for words. I knew that this was a child who had lost her body long ago, and with it whatever sense she had ever had of herself. To these children the act of sex is nothing, they have learned to separate head from body. They only know how to survive on a daily basis by getting money out of men. Yet sometimes their hearts speak, and I know, from my experience, how dangerous it is if they allow themselves to be children, to become vulnerable again. Then they are ashamed of what they have done, and the shame is dreadful.

Children like this can never truly return to childhood. When it is gone it is gone. It doesn't matter what help they are given, nothing will bring it back. That loss will be with them for the rest of their lives, and they can only learn to live with it, to stop it determining which way their lives go. But they are always vulnerable, always fragile. The supports of the bridge are always shaky.

These thoughts and feelings went through me as I sat by Delga and held her hand. Tears often came to my eyes, and I knew I was grieving not just for her but for myself. Once she pushed me away and ran out of the apartment, and when she came back I knew she had been to the park to look for men. She had to do it. There was nothing else she knew.

I discovered that the beautiful child, Helga, loved to play the guitar, and I gave Nara the money to go and buy one. I know that some of the staff thought this was a ridiculous indulgence, and in Vietnam I am sometimes criticized for spoiling the Sunshine children. But to me a child's life is far more than clothes and food. It's spirits and souls too that need feeding and to me it was important that Helga should have a guitar. I had never ceased to be amazed by her beauty and her bearing. Her slanted eyes were like little black opals, but so lively, and when she smiled she smiled with her entire face.

We sat together all of us, on my last evening, and the children sang while Helga played. I had never heard children's voices like theirs. They were not like children's voices, but more profound, and the song they sang was like distant drums in the mountains, and like the wind moving across the steppe, natural, full of longing and ineffably sad. I simply sat and wept.

I was still hearing that music as I flew back to Vietnam.

TWENTY-SIX

Things moved fast in Mongolia. By September we had permission from the prison authorities to run literacy classes for twenty-four of the boys who couldn't read or write. We had also found two very experienced Mongolian teachers and they had set themselves the target of getting the children through to the end of third grade by the summer of 1998. Classes were to begin in October.

Staff had also been into both prisons to talk to the children and discover what subjects they themselves would like to learn. I believe children always do best if they are learning something they have chosen. Carpentry and electronics were top choices for the boys, and the girls wanted cookery and language classes, especially English. The prison authorities were willing, and classes there were scheduled to start in November.

News of the village had flashed around the area of Ulaanbaatar, and many women and children had arrived, asking to be taken in. It was a difficult situation. There were so many social problems in Ulaanbaatar, especially alcoholism, and if the village was to function properly we had to be selective. We only had limited space and we had to choose people we thought would be able to fit in.

Some of the *ger* family units were already settling down just as we'd hoped they would. Wendy described to me a woman in her fifties called Oyun, who they had come across living rough with her twelve-year-old daughter Basansuren in the entrance to one of the hospitals. Oyun had gradually been forced to sell everything after a series of deaths in the family – traditional funerals are important in Mongolia, and also very expensive. Oyun was completely destitute, but she was still doing her best for Basansuren. She had found some school books in a dustbin and had been trying to teach her from them.

The two had moved into the *ger* village, and within a week the staff had managed to get Basansuren into the local school. With her mother's help she was beginning to catch up on her missed lessons. Oyun was also being a real mother to the five other children living with them, and was embroidering curtains for all the *gers* in beautiful traditional designs.

Not all the stories were so happy. I had been haunted by the memory of Delga and her sisters since I'd left Mongolia. Caroline had become very attached to the twins and our social workers had eventually managed to make contact with their mother. Her husband was still beating her up and she was asked if she would like to leave him and make a home for the three children, so that they would no longer have to live on the streets.

The mother was very plausible. She cried buckets. Yes, yes, she badly wanted to leave her husband. She loved her children and there was nothing she would like better than to have them back.

So the Foundation arranged sponsorship for the family and rented them a small wooden house, or *hasha*, on the outskirts of Ulaanbaatar. But the idyll didn't last long. Within weeks a

192

neighbour reported to Wendy that they were damaging the *hasha*, and using it as a brothel. The girls were bringing men back at night and the mother was charging for the girls' services.

The staff in Mongolia were terribly upset to think the mother was acting as a pimp, and extremely worried about the girls. When they talked to her it was hard to establish the true facts, but it was clear she didn't really care about the children and the decision was made to stop the family's funding. It is always a painful thing to do, but if parents are involved in their children's prostitution there is very little hope that things will improve. The girls were offered places in the *ger* village, but they said they preferred to stay with their mother.

I was disturbed by the memory of the days I had spent with Delga. I remembered her small sad figure rocking, rocking as the tears coursed down her cheeks. I wished I was there to talk to her because I felt I might have been able to persuade her to move into the village. But now she and her sisters were again prostituting themselves on the streets.

I worried a lot about Mongolia, and sometimes I questioned myself about what we had taken on. I knew all of the staff were working far too hard, and life there was dangerous – unsavoury people moved about the streets of Ulaanbaatar, and there was always a possibility that staff would be attacked or children kidnapped. We had already had to increase the number of guards at the village. Our staff were dealing with damaged people and dislocated lives, and the situation was often very threatening.

In late summer a new visitor had arrived in Tu Xuong Street – a young Australian film-maker called Steven Jeffares, who had been given finance by ABC Television in Australia and by the Irish television station RTE to make a one-hour documentary. By now we had all begun to take the constant flow of visitors, film-makers and journalists in our stride, but this was something different. Steven Jeffares told me that to make his hour-long feature he would need to film at the Foundation for about five hundred hours.

'You must be joking!' I said.

'Well,' he said, 'filming with children is difficult. You want to catch them unawares. It's a bit like wildlife photography.'

I'd had a hard time travelling and I was very tired. I just wanted to hibernate now until Christmas, and the idea of having a film crew following me around for months appalled me. But then again, I thought, another documentary might buy us some new computers, and I liked what I'd seen of Steven Jeffares. So I agreed.

We weren't really used to this kind of constant surveillance, and Dan especially found the business of filming difficult. He kept forgetting the camera was running and wandering into shot. Just as the crew were beginning to film me a brown hand would loom across the viewfinder. It was Dan, handing me a piece of paper.

'Dan!' we would all exclaim in chorus, and Dan would apologize sheepishly. But Steven Jeffares was very relaxed and good-humoured, and usually we all ended up laughing. I became familiar with all the jargon and before long I was calling close-ups 'CUs' like any film buff.

Day after day the camera crew followed me around. They filmed me making phone calls, talking to the staff, playing with the children, and walking through the Saigon streets. One day I took them out to Hoc Mon to see Hai and his family. It required negotiation. Hoc Mon is the rubbish-tip of Saigon, a huge, evil-smelling area where foreign camera crews are not normally permitted to go. But eventually we were given permission to film at the tiny house where Hai's family lived. The weather was scorching, the smell was appalling, and as the camera crew worked the sweat simply poured off them.

As always, Hai and the other children in the settlement came running towards us down the rough path. It was great to see Hai running. The first time I had seen him he had been in a terrible way, his bladder and his urinary tract crushed by a huge dumper truck that had accidentally driven over him.

The night it happened, Hai and his family had been out sifting through the rubbish on the tip as usual – that's how the families in Hoc Mon literally scrape a living. They had managed to get Hai to hospital, but he was hovering between life and death. We were told about him at the Foundation, and he and his family had become part of our lives. Hai was thirteen now, a lovely bright-eyed little lad. His terrible wound had finally healed, though he would always be scarred.

While we were caring for Hai we'd also worked to get the family out of the poverty trap in which they'd been living. We'd helped his mother set up a little food stall, and his father had a bike and was finding work away from the dump. Hai and his brothers and sisters were going to school, and Hai told me he wanted to be a doctor.

As always Steven and his team were cheerful, tactful and professional, but I could see they were deeply affected by their visit to Hoc Mon. Back on the streets of Saigon they caused a lot of interest among the cyclo drivers who always love to get in on the action. 'America? America?' they would ask eagerly, pointing to the film crew. To them all film-makers were American. I remember one of the drivers preening his hair and jutting out his masculine jaw as he made his bid to be a film-star.

'Americans big talk, big dollar,' he told the crew. 'Russians no talk, no rouble.' Then he looked at me and grinned. 'Mama Tina big talk, no dollar,' he said.

Yes, that about summed it up.

TWENTY-SEVEN

THE CITY BEGAN to feel festive. Tet, the New Year festival at the end of January, is the great celebration in Vietnam, with dragon dancers and fireworks, but there are many Catholics in Saigon who celebrate Christmas. Carols come drifting out of the Cathedral and there is a big Christmas tree with lights in the square.

Everywhere I went in the Centre kids were running around cutting out cards and decorations, and the floor was strewn with coloured paper, scissors and sticky tape. The phone was ringing continuously – not just with emergencies but with messages from people who were coming to the party. Dan put his head round the door to say the big crate of toys that the American Women's Association in Singapore sends us every year had just been delivered. It's always full of lovely presents, beautifully wrapped, and I offered up a little prayer of thanks to the Man Above that it had actually arrived. In past years the crate had sometimes got held up at Customs and we hadn't been able to get it out in time.

As usual, our friends in the business community had helped us with gifts and prizes. We'd been given lots of colas and Walls

196

ice-cream and there were traditional Vietnamese rice dishes, cakes and sweets. Clowns and puppeteers were coming to entertain the children for free. There seemed to be piles of boxes and bunches of balloons everywhere.

A great big star had gone up on the front of the Medical Centre, and there was an enormous Christmas tree covered with lights and decorations in the hall. Helenita and the children were practising carols. There was huge excitement. The Manager of the New World Hotel had asked the choir to sing in the hotel lobby during Christmas week, and this was to be their first public appearance. The choir had only been going for twelve weeks, and it was hard for the children to turn up for extra rehearsals since most of them were working. So they only had the usual music lesson times to rehearse.

I sat in the office listening to the voices drifting up from the courtyard, remembering what trouble I'd got into for smuggling the children into the Rex Hotel when I first arrived in Saigon. And now they had actually been *invited* into the New World Hotel! Nine years ago I wouldn't have thought it possible. Helen Thuong came into the office with a thick red Father Christmas costume over her arm.

'You going to be Father Christmas, Mama?'

'Oh Helen,' I said, 'in this heat? Wouldn't someone else like to do it this year?'

'No. Children say they want you. All want Mama Tina,' said Helen, and she left the office decisively, draping the outfit over a chair.

We have a lot of parties at the Foundation. I was so deprived of celebrations when I was a child that I think I can never have enough of them, and I want the children to have good memories to make up for the bad ones, happiness to carry them through when times are hard. We celebrate anything there is to celebrate. We have Tet parties, New Moon parties, beginning of school parties, graduation parties, summer picnics, but for the Sunshine children the Christmas party is definitely Number One, and they get excited about it weeks beforehand.

On the day of the party the older children who've left the Sunshine School always start arriving to ask if they can help and join in the party. Our kids never leave us, even if we're out of touch for a while. They keep coming back, like a family, and I love that. On party day they fetch and carry, and take care of the little ones, and help put up big tables out in the compound.

I'm usually rushing round like a blue-arsed fly at Christmas, wrapping up last-minute gifts for the staff. I always make sure that every child has a proper present – not just a token, but something they're really going to like. We divide the boys and girls into groups according to their age, and thanks to our sponsors they get beautiful things – boxes of Lego and Scalextric, games, dolls – and there's always a big box of cuddly toys. Even our biggest children love toys to cuddle.

Christmas 1997 really was a wonderful party. It seemed as if everyone we knew in Saigon came – the British consul and other foreign diplomats, our friends from the government agencies, people from the women's organizations, business people who had become our supporters. We all sat together, staff and visitors and children. Children got up and used the tinny old microphone, and we sang carols that rang out right the way down Tu Xuong Street. Members of staff did little turns, which always sends the children into fits, and I sweltered in my Father Christmas outfit in a temperature of more than 90 degrees.

But the high point of Christmas was the Foundation's White Christmas Ball at the New World Hotel. The New World means something very special in Saigon. It was the first of the big modern Western-style hotels – all plush carpets and deep chairs and shiny wood and marble. When the New World was built it signalled the beginning of a new era in the city, a sign that outside investment was moving in.

We'd been talking for many months to Mr Catoire, the General Manager, about the arrangements for the ball. Mr Catoire is a charming Frenchman with a compassionate heart, and he was very enthusiastic about hosting this gala evening in aid of the Foundation. We'd decided we'd really push the boat out this year to make it an elegant occasion.

We managed to get everything donated, from the beef for the main course to the dessert wine, and we were given fabulous prizes for the raffle – air tickets to Europe from KLM, golfing weekends, holiday packages, and even a solitaire diamond from a diamond firm. Enterprise Oil gave us $600 for a fabulous Christmas hamper, and the New World Hotel donated a night in the Presidential Suite, with a dinner party for eight thrown in.

I was to be guest of honour at the ball. The staff and I had decided that there would also be two other special guests – Ha and Nghia, who would each be presented with a Gold Award for Achievement. We felt they had both shown exceptional courage and determination and it was time to give them both a real pat on the back.

Ha was reading and writing fluently now. He had moved on from his private lessons and gone to school, and he had become very good at maths. I still kept my eye on him because now and again he slipped a little – hanging out with bad company or having the odd drug on a Saturday night. But Ha and I had a very close relationship, and he listened to me, especially when he knew I disapproved. All in all he was a different boy from the tough little character everyone had wanted to give up on several years before, though I did worry about what he got up to when I was away.

Nghia was also a lad who had made the most of his chances. He was a gentle boy whose ambition was to go to art school and become a graphic artist, but his father had died, and his mother was sick and had no money. Recently he had been taken on by a construction firm who were giving him computer training, and he was doing well.

We decided to surprise Nghia and Ha with their invitations a few days before the ball, but I had already thought about what they were going to wear. I was determined they weren't going to look like poor relations – it is very important to me for the Sunshine children to be able to hold their heads up and feel they are as good as anyone else. Two of our sponsors had agreed to pay for made-to-measure evening suits, which of course you can get run up very quickly in Vietnam.

The choir had also got special outfits – adorable long white choir gowns with sunshine-yellow sashes. As Helen said, if you are a performer you need to feel really good in what you are wearing, and the children thought these outfits were absolutely wonderful. In fact once they'd tried them on it was hard to get them to take them off.

When I finally gave the boys their elegant invitations they were speechless with astonishment. Then anxiety set in.

'But Mama Tina,' said Nghia, 'what we wear? Many foreigners go there.'

'Don't you worry about that,' I said. 'Everything's been taken care of. You're going to have the works – made-to-measure evening suits, shirts and bow ties, the lot.'

Ha gave me his toothy grin. 'We can keep suit?' he asked.

'Of course you can,' I said. 'The suits belong to you. If you meet Mr Quoc here at ten tomorrow morning he'll take you downtown and get you fixed up. Bring your things around to my house about five on Saturday and you can get all dressed up there.'

On Saturday the boys arrived a good two hours early. I had been going through my wardrobe, wondering what on earth I was going to wear. Carefully, reverently, they took their suits out of the packaging and laid them on the spare bed. Then they retired to the shower where they spent the next hour or so splashing about, washing their hair and generally preening themselves. I could hear them talking and laughing excitedly as I got my well-worn shiny gold top and my faithful elastic-waisted black trousers out of the wardrobe. Would I be able to measure up?

As a finishing touch I'd bought each of the boys a bottle of toilet water, and they came out of the shower gleaming and highly scented. They disappeared into the bedroom. After a lot more talk and laughter, they finally appeared dressed and smiling, slightly awkward and almost unrecognizably hand-some. They could have been any two well-dressed boys ready for an evening out.

In fact to me they looked like princes, and I could feel the tears pricking my eyes as I went up to them and gave them each a kiss. I'd borrowed a couple of wristwatches to set off their outfits, and when I put Ha's on his wrist I noticed that even his battered hands were looking better. The handcream I'd bought him was obviously having an effect.

I have a long, free-standing mirror in my kitchen and the boys just couldn't stop looking at themselves. They strutted back-wards and forwards like two peacocks, moving this way and that, catching their reflections from every angle, adjusting a button here, pulling their cuffs down, lifting their heels up to look at the backs of their new shiny black leather shoes. They tweaked one another's bow ties, looked at one another's cuff-links, compared the tightness of their waistbands. They were barely ready to tear themselves away when Quoc at last arrived, looking extremely elegant in a well-fitting evening suit.

'My God, Quoc,' I said, 'it's a lucky woman who will grab you one day!'

'Thank you, Mama,' said Quoc graciously, his wide warm smile lighting up his face. 'You very beautiful too.'

We walked to the end of the lane where we picked up four Hondas to take us to the ball. Three handsome princes, I thought, and a fairy godmother dressed in trousers instead of a gown, and clutching a packet of cigarettes for a wand. We zoomed off in convoy through the neon lights and the pollution, and were dropped, rather unceremoniously, at the side entrance to the New World Hotel. Hondas aren't allowed at the front entrance, so we had to walk back around the block.

As we approached the entrance I could see Ha pulling down his cuffs and adjusting his bow tie rather nervously. Last time he'd got this near to a big hotel, when he was a scrawny little street child, he'd had a bucket of water thrown over him. Tonight, however, the uniformed doorman held open the door with a slight bow, and we entered the marbled lobby. We stood for a moment gazing up the grand staircase, which was decorated from top to bottom with white silk and satin ribbons and flowers.

Mr Catoire appeared, oozing charm and elegance in an Armani suit. He greeted me with open arms, and then shook hands warmly with Ha, Nghia and Quoc.

We mounted the stairs, which were heavy with the scent of flowers. At the top there was another reception committee consisting of Helen Lowy, the hotel's public relations manager who had done a tremendous amount to make the event a success, and Christine Byrne, now volunteer co-ordinator at the Foundation.

A waiter appeared to offer us champagne or orange juice from a silver tray. The boys accepted with dignity, though I requested my usual – a Coca Cola Light. Then we were caught up in the elegant crowd, people greeting and kissing, friends wishing us well. I caught sight of my three handsome young men, talking and raising their glasses in a very self-possessed manner.

I was so proud of the three of them at that moment, though as we moved into the long ballroom, I could see they were finding the splendour of the occasion a little overwhelming. Every wall of the long ballroom was draped with white satin, the ceiling was hung with satin, and the round tables and the chairs were covered in white brocade. In the centre of each table was an eight-branched candelabra with red candles which cast a flickering light on to the tiny silver and white place cards and the gleaming silver cutlery.

We were shown to the top table, and Ha and Nghia were seated on either side of me. On a stage at the end of the ball-room an orchestra was playing popular tunes against some snowy alpine scenery. Then the Sunshine Choir arrived to open the evening. They filed on to the stage very solemnly, looking like little angels in their gold and white gowns. They stood up very straight, with their feet in their brand-new shiny black shoes all neatly together. Their mops of dark hair were brushed and shining and by the time they'd finished the first carol, I don't think there was a dry eye in the house. They sang some carols in Vietnamese and some in English, opening their mouths wide, and singing their hearts out. At the end of their performance the youngest of them presented me with a bouquet and they left the stage in a highly professional manner to deafening applause.

After dinner the Master of Ceremonies for the evening made a speech. Then the three of us were called up on to the stage. I made a little speech about Nghia and Ha and presented them with their awards to enthusiastic applause from the assembled diplomats, officials from Hanoi and international business people. They stood beside me, their heads slightly bowed, looking as if they had been receiving awards all their lives, and Helen Lowy presented each of them with a bouquet.

After we had left the stage Bill Mackenzie, the general manager of Price Waterhouse in Vietnam, approached Ha and asked him to come for an interview the following week for a job as junior clerk. Ha was quite overcome, and I was delighted. As well as being highly professional, Bill is a family man, understanding but firm, and I knew that working for him could be the making of Ha.

Then the band struck up and the dancing started. I decided I'd go and congratulate the choir, so I set off down the thickly carpeted corridor to the room that had been set aside for them. Helen had quietly insisted that they should be treated in the same way as any other performers, and the New World Hotel had also laid on generous amounts of coke and ice-cream.

They weren't quite like any other performers, I must admit. The room was empty, but when I opened the door of the luxurious toilets I was hit by a blast of hot air and steam. There were the kids, shouting and jumping about all over the place, with every tap full on and hair-dryers going nineteen to the dozen. It was such an extraordinary sight I burst out laughing. A moment ago they'd looked as if butter wouldn't melt in their mouths, though of course I should have known better.

I asked them what they thought they were doing and they explained that the air-conditioning in the hotel was so cold, and their choir gowns were so thin, that they were freezing. They were just trying to warm themselves up. They had never seen toilets like these before and they were fascinated. They were stuffing luxury toilet rolls and soaps and flannels into their pockets and down their knickers and trousers. It looked as if locusts had been at the place.

After the final reckoning we found that the ball had raised $18,000 for the Foundation. I think it was our angelic choir that had persuaded people to dig deep into their pockets – so they were entitled to their fun.

Coming Home

TWENTY-EIGHT

CHRISTMAS WAS OVER and I sat in my old pink armchair gazing out of the window. The Saigon sky was a heavy tropical blue shading almost to violet – so different from the grey umbrella of the Dublin sky, so different from the cold blue skies of Mongolia. It had been a successful, happy Christmas, and yet I was wrung out. I felt a lump building in my throat, a pain around my heart, and I began to cry. I don't think I can remember a Christmas when I haven't cried. For some of us the memories and the losses are too much. Even now, with everything I had in the world, I felt that everyone belonged but me.

As I gazed out of the window, my mind was full of the sounds and smells of Marrowbone Lane – the sour waft of Guinness on my father's breath, the damp woollen smell of our vests drying on the old clothes-horse in front of the fire Mam always kept burning on Christmas Eve. We'd all sit round in the light of the fire, because more often than not we had no electric, and Mam would sing to us. You tried so hard, Mam. Why was there never anyone to help us, I kept thinking. Why did we never belong?

209

I remembered the good years when Mam got together the money to buy a bit of ham for Christmas. I saw her, balanced on one of our rickety chairs, sticking coloured streamers to the ceiling. 'Hand me it up now,' she'd say. She was so pleased, so determined that we were going to have a good time, but for me the happiness was spoiled. I knew Mam had borrowed the money and now she would have to pay it back. I didn't want the worry to make her ill again. Even as a small child I knew Mam was always worried.

It was very rare that there was money for toys. On Christmas Day the other children would be out on the streets, showing off their presents, riding their bicycles and scooters, playing with their dolls' prams, but we'd stay indoors. Oh Mam, I thought, I'm a mother now, and I know what that must have felt like. It must have broken your heart.

And then the terrible Christmas after Mam died. We were still together then, me and Sean and Kathy and little Philomena, they hadn't yet come to split us up and take us away. On Christmas Day we all huddled together in the bedroom, on the bare horsehair mattress with the big dip in the middle and all the springs sticking out. The electric and the gas were off, and we'd one thin little blanket between the four of us, and some smelly old overcoats piled on top. And the picture of the Sacred Heart of Jesus looking down at us from the wall above the bed. And Dad still drunk from the night before, his eyes all swollen and bloodshot and his mouth all crooked.

The snow was blowing in through the broken window, and there was nothing for us to do but stay on the bumpy old bed, and tangle our blue feet together to keep warm, and try and rock ourselves to sleep until Christmas was over, swallowed up in the big black hole of the year, like the icy water that came out of the green tap in the scullery and disappeared down the plug hole. I couldn't look at my brother's and sisters' faces. When our tears flowed, they flowed in silence. There was nobody to put a fire in the sitting-room grate now. There were just dead ashes, and we all knew that our old life, protected by Mam, had gone out with the fire.

Sometimes during the day we crept into the cold scullery with the big chipped white sink and the dribbling cold tap, and drank some water from one of the empty condensed milk tins on the slatted wooden draining board. There was nothing to eat, and we'd suck the dirty kitchen cloth, pretending it was food, or chip shreds of wood from the floorboards and chew them. And then the sickness and the agonizing cramps. Nobody who hasn't starved can know what real hunger is like.

I struggled with these memories as I sat in my chair, looking out of the window and seeing only images of the past. After that there had been good times, I kept reminding myself. The happy Christmases when the children and I were together in the little house in Woking, on our own at last and no longer fearful of Mario. I remembered how we used to cook a big Christmas breakfast, with sausages and eggs and bacon and fried bread. And then I'd be in the kitchen, getting the Christmas dinner, and the house full of the smell of turkey and roast ham, and the children laughing and coming in and out, not frightened any more that Mario would come and pick a fight with me and beat me up.

That had been beautiful. When I thought about the three of them, I began to cry again. They were spread across the world now – Helen here with me in Vietnam, Michael and Androula in England, Nicolas and Sara in Australia. I missed them and longed for us all to be together.

How could people be so rational about the past, I wondered. We're told to put it all behind us, and that's what I had tried to do. I really wanted to be calm and philosophical about it, to stand up tall and strong and say 'That's over now, I've grown out of all that.' But I couldn't kid myself. The past for me would never be over. All I could do was remind myself that today was different.

At the same time I knew, deep down, that healing was taking place. It had been going on for years, and it was still continuing. Perhaps one day there'd only be the scars. But this Christmas, as at all other Christmases, the wounds felt very open.

I thought of Tuan, one of the toughest little nuts in the Sunshine Choir and a real little mischief-maker. One day when the choir was rehearsing Tuan's hands had gone up to his face and he had started sobbing. The song they were singing was one about children all over the world, and how they were one big family, and it had been too much for Tuan, who had left his family several years before. Helen quietly took him aside and held his hand, and after a while he said, 'I miss my mother, I miss my mother.'

Helen didn't want Tuan to feel embarrassed because it's so important not to lose face in Vietnam, so she didn't say much, just let him know by her acceptance that it was all right to feel sad and cry. After the practice was over Tuan told us that he wanted to find his mother again, and we promised we would help him. He wanted to tell her about the Sunshine Choir, and about how he had nearly learned to read. I guess we all need someone we love to tell when we've got something to be proud of.

I thought about Munkhbat, still in prison in Ulaanbaatar. In the middle of December the Foundation had given a little party to celebrate the good progress the boys were making in their literacy and numeracy classes. After the fun was over, Munkhbat had written a note saying that this had been his happiest day, and then he had tried to hang himself. Fortunately one of the teachers missed him and got to him in time, and she spent that night in the prison with him. We knew now that this was not the first time Munkhbat had tried to commit suicide.

During the night Munkhbat told the teacher that he missed his mother and worried about her every day because she was crippled and had no one. The teacher promised to see what the Foundation could do to help her, and she also arranged for Munkhbat to be taken to see her. When he arrived at his mother's tiny house Munkhbat was overcome. The two of them fell into one another's arms, weeping, and then they talked for several hours. On the way back to prison Munkhbat said he would never try to kill himself again. Seeing his mother had made him realize how much she loved him and how much she needed his help.

How could we do these things to children, I thought. How could we celebrate Christ's birth when children were being born into a world that did this to them?

The phone rang. For a moment I just sat looking at it, I was so far away. Then I picked up the receiver and heard Una Henry's Irish voice. I was glad to hear her. She and Barbara had been working so hard on the Foundation in Ireland, getting it registered with the government, setting up a Board of Directors. Una always had something warm and practical to say.

'Hello, Christina. How are you? How was Christmas?'

'I'm fine, Una,' I said, making an effort to sound cheerful. 'You know what Christmas is like.'

Una can read people, and she could hear that I was sad.

'I do know,' she said. 'But I've something to tell you that might cheer you up.'

'What?' I asked.

'You're coming home. You're coming home to Ireland,' said Una.

'No I'm not,' I said, 'not for a while anyway, Una. I've so much on here and . . .'

'No, Christina, you don't understand,' said Una. 'Are you sitting down? Well, Mary McAleese has agreed to launch the Christina Noble Children's Foundation, officially, here in Ireland.'

Mary McAleese? The President? Oh please, Una, I thought.

'Oh yes?' I said. 'Don't tease me now, Una. I'm sorry, I'm not really in the mood.' How strange of Una to make up something like that, I thought. And so unlike her.

'No truly,' Una persisted. 'Please listen to me now. The President has agreed to launch the Foundation on 15 February, here in Dublin in that beautiful hall right beside Christ Church. Can you make it? You'd better. It's all been arranged.'

Now Una was rattling on, telling me the Lord Mayor of Dublin was going to be there, and Mary Black the singer, 'and Mark Mortel of the Irish Tourist Board is going to introduce you, and Luca Bloom who wrote that song "I'm Coming Home, Child" for your documentary for RTE and . . .' The list seemed endless. And I just sat there thinking, 'Is it possible, all these people turning out in the Great Hall at Christ Church for little Christina Byrne from Marrowbone Lane Flats . . . ?' Although I knew now that Una was serious, there was a part of me that couldn't quite believe that the President of Ireland could think it worth her while.

'Why would the President want to do that?' I said to Una rather stupidly.

'Well, they think you're something pretty special over here, you know,' said Una. 'Now, Christina, is that all right? Will we talk again in a day or so, and then I can tell you more about the arrangements. I must go, but put that on your calendar now – 15 February.'

'15 February,' I said. 'I'll put it on the calendar.' I went through to the kitchen and wrote it up in big red letters.

Then I picked up the phone again to tell Helen and Dan and everyone over at the Centre. I was crying again, but these were different tears. I did feel that I was truly coming home.

TWENTY-NINE

On St Valentine's Day 1998 I stood with my suitcase at Dublin Airport, feeling anxious. I always felt this way when I landed in Dublin. 'They've invited you. The President of Ireland is supporting you,' I kept telling myself, but no matter what I said, the old frightening tapes would keep playing.

I knew I'd feel better once I saw Una, but mysteriously she wasn't there. Perhaps something had gone wrong. Perhaps something had happened to Una. It was ridiculous how shaky I felt. I stood listening to the background of Irish voices, taking in the soft greys and browns of the scene, trying to make the mental adjustment I always have to make after the noise and colour of Vietnam. I sat on my case and smoked a cigarette. Twenty minutes ticked by. I smoked another.

Then I saw a flash of a red jacket and a pony tail and I knew it was Una. There was a familiar handsome streaked blond head beside her, rising above the crowd. The last time I'd seen that head it had been behind a camera – Steven Jeffares, my nice young film-maker. I knew why he was here. His film, *Mama Tina*, was going to be shown on television all over

216

Ireland on the night of the launch. I stumbled towards them with my suitcase, waving and shouting, and the three of us hugged – a strange sight since I only came up to Steve's waist and had to put my arms around his hips.

'Where have you been?' said Una. 'We've been waiting and waiting.'

'Well, you must have been in the bar then,' I said.

We all laughed. I suddenly felt warm and safe, a tremendous release of tension. Una drove me to the Killiney Castle Hotel, where the management had kindly invited me to stay. As we sat in the comfort of my room Una outlined the major events.

'Tomorrow there's the launch with the President. That'll take about three hours. Then on Tuesday Christ Church. Wednesday it's Derek Ryan and Thursday there's your talk in Wexford . . . Cork . . . radio show . . . Limerick . . . lunch . . . talk . . . Castlebar . . . Sligo . . . bit of a rest . . . Saturday . . . Longford . . . Athlone . . . Mullingar . . . Kilk . . .' Una's warm voice murmured on, and I could feel myself sinking, deeper, deeper, my eyes closing.

'And then of course when you get back to Dublin you'll have a few days to yourself.' I jerked myself awake. 'And now you must get your rest,' said Una, rising.

It may have been partly my disturbed body-clock, and the discomfort in my joints after the long flight, but it seemed to be a feeling of awful anxiety that woke me a few hours later. I just lay there wondering who the hell I was and what I was doing. Tomorrow I was going to be received by the President of Ireland. That was great. It was a recognition not just for my work but for the Foundation, the children and everyone who was part of it. But what was happening to me? Was I just going to live the rest of my life as a fund-raiser, travelling restlessly around the world?

I felt trapped and anxious, little Christina Byrne again, at the mercy of forces I seemed unable to control. And tomorrow I was going to see Sean. My brother Sean had been so fired by what I was doing that he was setting up an office for the Foundation in Zurich, and he was flying over tomorrow for the Irish launch.

So much past and so much present, all mixed in together. I switched on the bedside light. It was after eleven. I wondered what I could do to calm myself. I realized what I needed was some nice fish and chips. I suddenly felt ravenously hungry. I dialled room service.

The female voice was apologetic. 'Everything's shut down now, I'm afraid.'

A few minutes later there was a genteel bleeping.

'Hello, Miss Noble. Our General Manager says he'd be delighted to go out and get you some fish and chips. He's sure he can find some somewhere.'

'What, Mr Brennan? That's a lot for him to do.'

'Sure he's delighted to do it.'

Ireland. This could only happen in Ireland.

'Is it just fish and chips you want, or is there anything else?'

'No, just fish and chips. But could you make sure they've plenty of salt and vinegar on them?'

'I certainly will.'

After a while there was a loud knocking. I opened the door to a waiter with a large silver-domed dish. He glided in and lifted the lid. Beneath it on a china plate embossed with the hotel crest were the fish and chips. They were steaming hot and I could smell the salt and vinegar. Beside them on the tray was a small glass with a single rose. I felt royal.

'With the compliments of the General Manager,' said the waiter. They were the best fish and chips I'd ever tasted.

*

218

I stopped to look at myself again before I went downstairs next evening to meet Una. It's not often I look in a mirror, and even less often that I'm pleased with what I see, but I knew I was looking nice. I was wearing a long green velvet dress I'd had made in Saigon. No one could know it had only cost me $20. My hair was held back in a bun circled with a green velvet band edged in gold. I knew that it suited my blonde hair. I felt good.

We drove through the city and past the great grey arched gate of Dublin Castle where the Children's Court is. Sean and Philomena and Kathy and I had been driven through that gate the day we'd been taken into care. The day we'd been driven away like criminals in the Black Maria, and our daddy had let them do it without a murmur, just turned and walked away. That was the day I'd finally given up on big people. I pushed the bad memories back.

In the Great Hall, with its glorious stained-glass windows, a big crowd was seated. I was introduced to the Lord Mayor, and then the President arrived. She clasped my hand. I was struck by her looks, so tall and slim and elegant, but most of all by her warm, kind eyes. Mary McAleese might be President of Ireland, but as we talked I knew that she was a mother first and foremost, a person who truly cared about the dispossessed of the world.

We walked together round the exhibition of photographs of the Sunshine children in Mongolia and Vietnam, and the President looked carefully at them all, genuinely interested. Then I gave her a present – a special picture painted by Hanh, our gifted artist from the Sunshine School. It was an out-pouring of glorious colour, the very texture of Hanh's soul, the stuff her dreams were made of, and as I told the President about Hanh I could see that she was deeply moved.

After a welcome, the Director of the Irish Tourist Board,

Mark Mortel, invited me on to the podium. I felt as if I was in some kind of dream – it all seemed so unreal that I wasn't even nervous. But as I began to speak about the evils and injustice children face in the world, I caught sight of Sean. His head was slightly bowed, but he was looking straight at me, and I knew I was speaking for all of us – myself and him and all my brothers and sisters, and all the voiceless children whose lives have been blighted by cruelty and poverty and injustice.

Then Mary McAleese spoke. She said many wonderful things, but the words that stayed in my mind were these. 'My grandmother always said to me: "One life lived well can make a difference." And your life, Christina, has made a colossal difference. I don't think that anyone could have had a better name to do the work that you do, bringing true nobility and true dignity to the lives of children who would otherwise perhaps not know what noble and dignified individuals are.'

That is what I had wanted to do, to make a difference, to give back dignity to children whose dignity had been taken away. If I had lived my life well in doing that, lived up to my name, then I was happy.

All through that evening I had a wonderful feeling of rightness, of being in a place where I belonged at last. Tonight I knew was important not just for the Foundation but for all the O'Byrne family. We might be spread all over the world, but our souls were Irish and always would be. I realized how passionately I wanted my children and my children's children to know that they had roots – not to feel like strangers in Ireland as I had done for so long.

I was given a special tour of Christ Church Cathedral, and I had a new feeling of belonging as the curator courteously showed me round. We walked through the beautiful twelfth-century cathedral where the great Strongbow is buried, and saw the excavated remains of the Viking city. I remembered being told by my daddy that the O'Byrnes had been kings in Wicklow. 'This is my history,' I kept thinking, 'I'm part of all this and all this is part of me.'

Sean and I sat together in the hotel lounge. We both felt too emotional to say much. In all the years since we had been parted we had never really spoken about what had happened to us. The memory had always been too painful. I knew the bare facts of what had happened to Sean. He had been sent to a reform school in Dublin run by the Christian Brothers, Artane, and then to their notorious so-called industrial school at Letterfrack.

When he was fifteen Sean had escaped from Letterfrack and made his way to Dublin. He had lived rough on the streets, hiding from the authorities and earning a few pennies by carrying sacks in the markets and delivering groceries. Eventually he had managed to travel to Germany, where our eldest brother, Michael, was living.

Like Sean I had been put into a Dublin institution on that day. I had escaped too, and for a while lived rough in Phoenix Park, before being sent to St Joseph's, only eight miles from Letterfrack. What had happened when the nuns finally let me go had been like a branding with a hot iron – the months of living rough like a hunted animal, the gang rape, Thomas's birth and the day they had taken him away. These things would be with me always, I knew, though even now I could hardly bear to speak of them.

Philomena and Kathy had grown up in another orphanage. When I left Ireland, I knew that they were alive, but it was only when I saw our other brother Andy, in Birmingham, that I found out Sean was still living. When he and I made contact again it was as if we had both come back from the dead.

221

That is what we were then, I thought, like ghosts, trying to find a way back into the world. Somehow we had all survived. Kathy and Philomena now lived in England, and Sean had settled in Zurich. I knew that the name of his pub 'The Noble Dubliner' was a compliment to me.

Sitting with him now, in this city where we saw our past in every street, was painful. I could hardly bear to look at Sean. Instead of a gentle, greying man of fifty I kept seeing a fair-haired little boy with dirty clothes and dirty feet, and a dirty tear-streaked face. 'Promise you won't let them keep me, Ina,' he was saying, 'promise you won't let them keep me.' I'd promised him, but I hadn't been able to keep my promise.

After a long silence Sean said, 'I heard some years back they'd closed Letterfrack. My God, Ina, what a place.'

His hands on the arms of his chair were trembling. The muscles of his jaw were working, and tears began to run down his face.

'Can you tell me about Letterfrack?' I said, carefully. 'Can you tell me what happened at Artane?'

'I don't know if I can, Ina,' said Sean. 'I think I'm afraid to open the door. Even now I can't bear anyone to touch me. I can shake hands, but that's about all.'

He took a deep, quivering breath. 'I can't really tell you the horror of those places. We were starving. When I was at Artane we had two pieces of bread in the morning and just slops for lunch. You'd often find cockroaches in it. Then a couple of pieces of bread in the evening, and that was it.

'You were so hungry you got cramps in your stomach. Sometimes I was so hungry I'd ask for some more, but you didn't dare to do that very often. One of the Brothers, a big fat slob, would whack you across the face and head if he was in a bad mood.

'I was so desperate once I broke into the kitchen and ate

some onions. One of the Brothers smelt them on my breath and he took me out and punched me like a criminal. There was froth coming out of his mouth, I remember. He called me and Mam and Dad and all of us every filthy degrading name he could think of.

'They were so violent, Ina. Talk about Christian. They'd punch you and lash you with a leather strap, bend you over and lift up your clothes and beat you until you just kept begging them to stop. Just begging for mercy. Your legs and your bottom afterwards would be nothing but pain. They'd pull your hair till you screamed your heart out. They loved it. They gloated. What the fuck was their problem? How in God's name can these people live with their consciences? Nothing will ever excuse what they did.'

Sean was weeping openly, and I knew how angry he was too. It takes a lot to make Sean swear. 'I think everything they did was meant to humiliate you,' he said. 'We only got a change of underclothes every two weeks, but they'd come and inspect to see if you were keeping your pants clean and if they found the slightest mark they'd beat you and ridicule you in front of the other children. We had one shower a month in freezing water, and foot-washing was twice a month.

'You know I escaped out of there many times, but some-body always squealed on me and the police would take me back.'

'Where did you go?' I said. 'How did you live?'

'I went back to Marrowbone Lane,' said Sean. 'I slept on the landings in the flats, in the corners of those concrete stairs where some of the kids used to piss. Oh that smell, I hated it. I'd go and sleep in the old dirty sheds and rubbish dumps. Sometimes I'd take milk bottles from people's doorsteps. I even stole a cake once, with pink icing on and fruit inside. I didn't want to, but I didn't know what else to do.'

'If only I'd known,' I said. 'I must have been living out in Phoenix Park when you were back in the Lane. If only I'd known, I'd have come and found you. What do you think we'd have done then?'

'Robbed two bottles of milk and two pink cakes with fruit inside,' said Sean, and we both started laughing. Just for a minute we were two kids again, back in the Liberties.

'How many times did you get out of Artane before they sent you to Letterfrack?' I asked.

'It must have been after the twelfth time,' said Sean. 'I had to go in front of the judge. He said "I'm sending you to a place you won't be able to escape from".'

'Was Letterfrack just as bad?'

'Oh, it was worse,' said Sean. 'I got out of there too, in 1960 I think the first time was, when I was thirteen. I jumped the wall and the Brothers ran after me. They got some of the older boys and they cornered me like a rat. I was so frightened, I felt such terror, I ran right out into the Atlantic. Oh my God it was cold, and wild. You know what the ocean's like out there in the west.

'They pulled me out and the Brothers punched me and kicked me. Then they made me stand up against the wall in the yard all day with my wet clothes on. No one was allowed to speak to me, and I wasn't given any food. When they let me take off my clothes I was blue with cold, I was shivering so much I couldn't stop. Then they made me take my shoes off and walk round and round the yard barefoot.

'That night the other boys weren't allowed to do their sports. We used to have a game once a week, and the Brothers told them it was a punishment because Sean Byrne had run away. So then none of the boys would speak to me. I wasn't ever allowed to play in the game after that.'

It was terrible to listen to all this. I felt sick with anger that men who called themselves Christian had done these things to Sean, little Sean, my brother, whose only crime was that his mother had died. My God, I thought, the evil in those places. How had we come through? How had we been so strong?

'After that they hated me,' said Sean. 'They shaved my head, and one time one of the Brothers made me lie across my bed on my belly. He had a thick leather belt, and he lifted my night things and lashed me with it, oh, twenty-five or thirty times. Another time he made me take off my clothes in the wash-room. Then he turned the lights out and just left me. I was naked, Ina, just standing there in the dark. They took all your dignity away.

'When the dormitory lights went out one of the Brothers often used to come and tell the pretty-looking boys they had to come outside to see someone. We all knew what that meant. They were only young kids, ten, eleven, twelve. I used to look in their eyes next morning and they looked dead and lost. I was always waiting for my turn, but luckily for me I wasn't so pretty.

'They took me out of school and put me to work painting people's houses. I had to work like a slave on the farms, from dawn till after ten at night. Did somebody get money for that? I never did.

'In the end I got sick with pneumonia. They left me till it was almost too late, and then they had to rush me into Galway, to the hospital. I think they were worried I was going to die.'

'Thank God, Sean,' I said. 'Thank God you didn't.'

'I often used to wish I was dead,' said Sean. 'I never had a visitor in all those two years. I was so lonely. Oh, Ina, I missed you. When I got out and went to look for you at St Joseph's the nun who came to the door told me you were dead. I didn't have anything left to live for then. I never let them see me cry, but I was broken. I'd no hope left. But after all that I did get away.'

'There weren't many who did that,' I said. 'Not many ever escaped from Letterfrack.'

'How did we ever survive?' asked Sean.

'I don't know,' I said. 'I don't know.'

'But we did, Sis. Up yours, Letterfrack, is what I say!'

'And up yours too, St Joseph's!' I said.

THIRTY

W HEN IRISH HEARTS are happy,
    all the world is bright and gay
And when Irish eyes are smiling,
      sure they'd steal your heart away . . .

I felt warm and contented as Una and I sped along through the Irish countryside on my fund-raising tour, singing as we went. Yet all the time deep emotions kept surfacing, and I was grateful that I was with Una, who simply seemed able to understand without any explanations.

On the way down to Wexford we were driving along between quiet green fields, and I looked across the countryside with its rivers and valleys to the blue-grey mountains in the distance, and a great sob rose up from my stomach, a deep sobbing. I cried and cried as if I'd go on for ever. Outside Dungarvon Una stopped the car.

'Would you like to get out,' she said, 'and look at the beauty of the land?'

'Yes.'

We walked along a little, with the mountains behind us, and

a breeze coming in from the sea. 'Una,' I said, 'this is Ireland. The Liberties and the schools of correction, they're not Ireland. *This* is what Ireland is.' I was still crying, for Sean and all of us and the pain of the past, and the bitter sweetness of the present, with all its unanswered questions.

In Dublin a young man with the greenest green eyes had come up to me after my talk. He seemed nervous, but he spoke very directly.

'Are you still looking for your son?' he asked.

I could feel my heart beating in my throat, and my breath was uneven.

'Why do you ask?' I said.

He didn't answer, but there seemed to be some strange connection between us.

'Can I ask your name?' I said. I almost expected him to say 'Thomas'.

'Joe. Just call me Joe,' he said. 'I'm afraid I have to go now. I'll be in touch with you again.'

'Let me give you an address to contact me,' I said quickly, and I scribbled down the address of the Foundation and gave it to him.

'Thanks,' he said. He gave me a long look. Then he turned abruptly and walked away.

I wanted to run after him, but I felt stupid.

Next afternoon I was talking to Lucia Ennis in the Dublin office. I described the young man and my meeting.

'That's very strange,' she said. 'I'm sure it was the same man. He came in this morning and gave quite a lot of money. He didn't want to leave his name or address or anything. He just said "I'll be in touch every once in a while".'

Una took me by the hand and walked me back to the car. 'You do know that one day you're going to come home and live here, don't you? That little dream house will be waiting for you one day.'

'Oh yes,' I said, smiling. 'And I'll have a little pig, and some chickens and ducks, and an Aga and a big pine table. It'll be lovely, like a dream, and everyone will come and visit me.'

The last night of the tour, in Kilkenny, was glorious. I walked into the ballroom of the New Park Hotel expecting to give a talk, and was greeted by the Kilkenny Children's Orchestra playing 'Danny Boy'. I looked round the audience, and it was full of faces I knew – friends from all over Ireland, even a friend from Germany and another from Vietnam. It was a surprise that the Irish Foundation had laid on for me.

I got up on the stage and gave a talk, and then afterwards I burst into song, and everyone sang along with me, all the old Irish favourites, and all the songs I used to sing back in Marrowbone Lane when I was dreaming of the day I'd go to Hollywood, 'Walking My Baby Back Home' and all the rest of them. It was grand. We had a great hooley.

Four days later I stood in Mount Jerome Cemetery in Dublin, in the place where I'd stood when I was ten years old as they lowered my Mam into a pauper's grave. She had no headstone, no memorial. But I had vowed then that one day I would give her one. And now, with the help of a kind woman called Oonah Linehan I had carried out my vow. Oonah had spoken to the stonemason at Mount Jerome and, for no fee, he had made a beautiful stone. On it I had asked him to write:

MAMMY
YOU LEFT US THE GREATEST GIFT OF ALL
'LOVE'
NOW YOU CAN SLEEP WITH PEACE
YOUR CHILDREN

The stonemason had cleaned and tidied the grave for me, and I scattered yellow daffodils and blue irises like a bedcover over Mam.

I didn't want anyone to come to the airport with me. I just wanted to slip quietly away. I'd kept my promise to Mam, and Sean I knew had begun his healing. Now, once again, I must find my own.

All the way back to Vietnam I could hear the music of the Kilkenny children in my ears. As the taxi drew up outside Tu Xuong Street I remembered the day I'd first seen the big gates of the compound, and heard the sound of children crying from behind the high wall. There were sounds now, all around the compound, different sounds. People talking, children laughing. 'Mama Tina! Mama Tina!' They came rushing out to meet me.

I went inside.

Epilogue

It is the summer of 1998 and I have spent most of the past six months travelling again – England, Ireland, France, Australia, Mongolia, Japan, and in a few weeks I shall be in New Zealand. The Foundation is registered in fourteen countries now. We're thinking of extending the Sunshine School again, and the Medical Centre. This year we opened a girls' shelter, and we're raising money to build a proper music school.

In Mongolia the *ger* village is flourishing, and early this year the Mongolian government showed its appreciation by giving us outright the land on which it stands. Helga, the little guitar player, is living there happily now, and three of the children from the sewers have been reunited with their families. But Delga and her two sisters are with their mother and still, we think, involved in prostitution.

When I was in Ireland I was given a wonderful present for Mongolia. Our friends at Mercedes, Derek Ryan and Matt Fagan, got together a special team to design and build an insulated 'Unimog', with sixteen gears and a tank body. It can go up mountains and through deserts, and we can use it as an ambulance if we need to. As well as protecting everyone against the fearful extremes of the Mongolian climate it helps us to reach nomad families in the Gobi Desert who are suffering terrible malnutrition and health problems.

We are still running classes for the children in prison, and after Christmas eight boys who had just been released sent me a letter:

Dear Mama Tina

We say you we sad we did commit a crime and were in the prison. But we know we very lucky to be given a chance to learn. We never heard in our life that anybody care to teach children in prison and having a good teaching. We think in the prison nobody remember bad boy. But you send many teacher here and we happy you remember. Now we no sad. You make this for us and we know even you so far away we love you.

We say Mama Tina you we love. And we wait you come back to Mongolia and we give you gift from work we do now. Thank you, you give back our life to us. Now we work hard to be good boy.

Love you, from boys came for the prison.

I shall see the boys soon when I go to Mongolia. There is still a lot to do there, and we are concerned about Dr Boshigtt. He has been on hunger-strike in the main square in Ulaanbaatar as a protest against the appalling conditions in the countryside. Mongolia can't afford to lose such a good man.

I've just been up in Scotland, where I visited the Hunts. In January 1998 Nguyen Tan Lap's adoption was officially approved by the Scottish authorities. Margaret and Robert's devotion has transformed Lap. He goes to mainstream school, and does art classes, and hydrotherapy is helping him to move more easily. Lap is healing himself on love.

And what of the other Sunshine children? Ha is getting married, he's found his darling, and he's still working at Price Waterhouse. Nghia has got his scholarship to art school. Le Le is happy in the children's centre at Ca Mau. The Sunshine Choir and Orchestra have become famous, and the Sunshine Football Team has been having a great time travelling around Vietnam.

There are sad endings too, of course. Lam is still on the streets, selling himself to the hideous paedophiles who come to Saigon to buy and abuse children, and so is Nam. Mai went back to live with her mother and her little brother and through friends of the Foundation she even got her beautiful dress with red roses and her new butterfly bike. Mai went back to school but she didn't stay, and now I fear for her future. I see her down in Pham Ngu Lao all dressed up and I don't like to think where her money is coming from.

As for my beautiful family, Helenita, Androula and Nicolas, they and their partners are still supporting me all the way. Nicolas is working full-time for the Foundation, and he and Sara are moving to Saigon. Michael and Androula are living and working in England, but we are always in contact and they give me such good advice. Helenita is still in Saigon, making music with the children. Last year she fell in love and married Craig Derbyshire, who had left his work in the theatre to travel in Vietnam. The kids love Craig and he is helping us set up a Sunshine Sports Project.

One important member of the family has not appeared in this story. Like me, Helenita gave birth to a son when she was young and she called him Thomas, knowing nothing at that time of the Thomas that I had lost. This lovely grandson of mine brings the story full circle. Unlike the rest of us he has grown up with love and security all around him and Thomas and I are very close.

When I am in England now I live on the south coast. This morning I looked out at the sea, and felt the wind on my face and listened to the seagulls, and I thought how lucky my life has been, and how thankful I am that I can enjoy this beauty. It's true, there is always too much to do and never enough time to do it in. The world still abuses its children in terrible ways. We still desperately need money, and sponsors for the children, especially in Mongolia, and sometimes I wonder where it is all going to come from.

But then I remind myself that when I first arrived in Vietnam I didn't have a penny. So my motto is still 'Never Say Never', and when I get together with the Sunshine children our favourite song, our signature tune, is still 'We Have a Dream.'

CHRISTINA NOBLE
CHILDREN'S FOUNDATION

Only through donations from people who
care can we continue our work in helping
the children of Vietnam and Mongolia. If
you would like to make a donation or
sponsor a child, you will find the address of
your nearest Foundation office on the
following pages.

GLOBAL OFFICES

AUSTRALIA
PO Box 548
Sutherland
NSW 2232
Tel: 61 295 282157
Fax: 61 295 282157
E-mail: vpe@ar.com.au
or australia@cncf.org

BELGIUM
Generaal Drubbelstraat 110
B2600 Ber Chem
Bercham
Tel: 32 3 218 5709
Fax: 32 2 762 6781
E-mail: patsc@glo.be
or belgium@cncf.org

CANADA
C/- Canadian Food for the Hungry
#005–2580 Cedar Park Place
Abbotsford, BC V2T 3S5
Tel: 1 604 853 4262
Fax: 1 604 853 4332
E-mail: cfh@mindlink.bc.ca

FRANCE
26 rue du Bouloi
75001 Paris
Tel: 33 1 40266993
Fax: 33 1 42334498
E-mail: mellet@club-internet.fr
or france@cncf.org

GERMANY
Maximillansplatz 10
Munchen 80333
Tel: 49 89 290 4747
Fax: 49 89 290 4746

HOLLAND
Weteringstraat 27
1017 SL Amsterdam
Tel: 31 20 6276577
Fax: 31 20 4222731
E-mail: rleyds@worldonline.nl
or holland@cncf.org

HONG KONG
14B Verdant Court
Discovery Bay
Lantau Island
Tel: 852 2649 2571
Fax: 852 2649 2571

IRELAND
Unit 2307, Richmond Business
Campus,
North Brunswick Street, Dublin 7
Mailing Address:
PO Box 5775, Dublin 4
Tel: 353 1 807 2448
Fax: 353 1 872 6252
E-mail: Una.Henry@boi.ie
or ireland@cncf.org

JAPAN
Building Shirogane # 101
2–2–18
Kamiohsaki
Shinagawa-ku
Tokyo 141
Tel: 81 33 280 4284
Fax: 81 33 280 4285
E-mail: cwolfson@gol.com
or japan@cncf.org

MONGOLIA (mailing address)
PO Box 74
Post Office 48
Ulaanbaatar
Tel: 976 1 322275
Fax: 976 1 322275
E-mail: cncfmongolia@magicnet.mn
or mongolia@cncf.org

SWITZERLAND
PO Box 8021
Zurich
Tel: 41 1 735 2166
Fax: 41 1 483 0461
E-mail: 101771.2734@compuserve.co
or switzerland@cncf.org

UNITED KINGDOM
10, Great George Street
7th Floor
London SW1P 3AE
Tel: 44 171 233 1413
Fax: 44 171 233 1424
E-mail: cncf@nol.co.uk
or uk@cncf.org

USA
305 Filbert Street
San Francisco, 94133
California
Tel: 1 415 956 7257
Fax: 1 415 421 4124
E-mail: usa@cncf.org

VIETNAM (mailing address)
PO Box 386
Saigon Post Office Center
Ho Chi Minh City
Tel: 848 8203484
Fax: 84 8 8222276
E-mail: cncfvn@saigon.teltic.com.vn
or vietnam@cncf.org

INTERNET HOMEPAGE ADDRESS:
http://www.cncf.org

Bank Account: International Account

Account Name: The Christina Noble Children's Foundation (HK) Ltd

Account No: 139-4-013112

Address: Hongkong Bank
                 The Hongkong and Shanghai Banking Corporation Limited
                 Bank No. 6
                 1/F Shatin Galleria
                 Shan Mei Street
                 Fo Tan
                 Hong Kong